Independent Dictionary

Ginny Lapage

Introduction

This is the third dictionary in a series for Emergent, Early and Independent readers. It has been devised with the active help of the children and teachers of a primary school who were involved at all the stages of compilation. The children made suggestions as to how the words should be defined or explained and the compiler made adjustments to meet their needs. The aim of a dictionary is to assist with spelling and to help with understanding. The series of three dictionaries have been designed to lead children in stages into using more formal dictionaries. The books are well illustrated and the definitions are given in full sentences. These dictionaries are intended to be fun as well as to give information.

The Independent Dictionary provides the stepping stone between the dictionary for the very young and the more conventional dictionary. It contains more than 2400 entries based on the vocabulary of the more independent reader (7–9 years old). The definitions cover all the usages of the words relevant to the young reader with the intention of raising awareness that a word can be used in many ways. It shows each word in its most common context as well as showing a wider range of meanings. The forms of the nouns, verbs, adjectives and adverbs are given in full to help spelling.

Ginny Lapage is an experienced primary school teacher. She has an M.A. in Children's Literature and a Diploma in Reading and Language Development. She has compiled the *Collins Junior Dictionary*, the accompanying workbook and the workbooks for the *Collins Picture Dictionary* and the *Collins Primary Dictionary*.

How to use this dictionary

A dictionary tells you the meaning of a word and how to spell it.

The guideword tells you the first and last word on each double page.

The headword is the word you want to know more about.

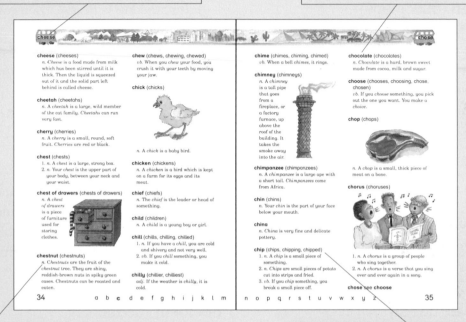

This shows the part of speech in its short form:

n. = noun   *vb.* = verb
adj. = adjective   *adv.* = adverb

This shows the different ways of using and spelling the word.

If you want to find a word, you need to think about the letter the word begins with. If you want to look up **cherry** you turn the pages until you come to the letter **c**. There are lots of **c** words. How can you find **cherry** without looking at every one? Look at the second letter of **cherry**. It is **h**. Keep looking through the pages until you come to the guidewords beginning with **ch** and you will find **cherry**.

If you want to know more about the parts of speech, look at pages 228 and 229.

A a

abdomen (abdomens)

n. Your *abdomen* is the part of your body that contains your stomach.

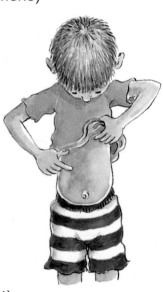

able (abler, ablest)

1. *adj.* An *able* person is good at doing things.
2. *adv.* When you are *able* to do something, you can do it.

aboard

adv. If you are *aboard* a ship or a bus, you are on it.

about

1. If it is *about* six o'clock, it is almost six o'clock.
2. If you watch a programme *about* cats, it tells you things to do with cats.

3. If someone is *about*, they may be anywhere around.

above

1. *Above* is overhead.
2. If you are *above* something, you are higher up.

absolutely

adv. If you say that someone or something is *absolutely* wonderful or absolutely dreadful, you mean that they are completely wonderful or completely dreadful.

accident (accidents)

1. *n.* An *accident* is something bad which happens when it is not meant to.

2. *n.* An *accident* is something which happens by chance.

accidentally

adv. If you do something *accidentally*, you do not mean to do it.

acid (acids)

n. *Acid* is a dangerous liquid that can burn your skin and clothes.

acorn (acorns)

n. An *acorn* is the seed of an oak tree.

across

If you go *across* a road or a river, you go from one side to another.

actor (actors)

n. A person or animal that performs in a play is called an *actor*. A woman or girl who performs in a play or film is called an *actress*.

actual

adj. *Actual* means the real thing.

add (adds, adding, added)

1. vb. If you *add* one thing to another, you make it bigger.

2. vb. If you *add* two or more numbers together, you find out the total.

admirable

adj. If someone's behaviour is *admirable*, people think it is very good.

admiral (admirals)

n. An *admiral* is an important officer in the navy.

adult (adults)

n. An *adult* is a grown-up.

advertise (advertises, advertising, advertised)

vb. When shops or companies *advertise*, they tell you about the things they want to sell so that you might buy them.

advertisement (advertisements)

n. An *advertisement* is a picture, writing or a very short programme on the radio or television which tells you about something a shop or a company wants to sell.

aeroplane (aeroplanes)

n. An *aeroplane* is a machine that flies. It can carry passengers or goods.

afloat

adj. If something is *afloat*, it is resting on the top of the water.

afraid

adj. If you are *afraid*, you are scared or worried about something.

after

1. *adv.* When you do something *after* something else, you do it later.
2. *adv.* If something happens *after* something else, it happens next.

afternoon (afternoons)

n. The *afternoon* is the time of day between midday and evening.

afterwards

adv. If something happens *afterwards*, it happens later.

again

adv. When you do something *again*, you do it once more.

against

1. If you are *against* something, you do not agree with it.
2. If you put one thing *against* another, you put it on or next to it.

ago

adv. If something happened a few days *ago*, it happened in the past.

agree (agrees, agreeing, agreed)

vb. If you *agree* with someone, you think the same way as they do.

agreement (agreements)

n. If you make an *agreement*, you arrange with someone to do something.

ahead

adv. If someone or something is *ahead*, they are in front.

air

n. *Air* is all around you but you cannot see it. You need air to breathe.

aisle (aisles)

n. An *aisle* is a pathway between rows of seats. There are aisles in churches, aeroplanes and cinemas.

alien (aliens)

n. An *alien* is a creature that comes from another planet.

alike

>   *adj.* When two things are *alike*, they are like one another.

alive

>   1. *adj.* If something is *alive*, it is not dead.
>   2. *adj.* If something or someone comes *alive*, they seem to wake up.

alley (alleys)

>   *n.* An *alley* is a narrow street or passageway between or behind buildings.

alligator (alligators)

>   *n.* An *alligator* is like a crocodile but it has a shorter and broader jaw and bigger teeth. *Alligators* live in lakes and rivers in America and China.

allotment (allotments)

>   *n.* An *allotment* is a small piece of land that people pay rent to use. Fruit, flowers and vegetables are grown on *allotments*.

allow (allows, allowing, allowed)

>   *vb.* If you *allow* someone to do something, you let them do it.

almost

>   *adv.* If you have *almost* done something, you have nearly done it.

alone

>   *adj.* If you are *alone*, you have no-one with you.

along

>   If you go *along* a path, you go from one end to the other.

already

>   *adv.* If you have done something *already*, you did it earlier.

always

>   *adv.* If you *always* do something, you do it again and again.

amazing

>   *adj.* If something is *amazing*, it is surprising and unusual.

ambulance (ambulances)

>   *n.* An *ambulance* is a special vehicle that is used to take people to hospital.

among or **amongst**

If you are *among* the trees or *amongst* a crowd of people, you are in the middle of them.

ancient

adj. Something that is *ancient* is very, very old.

anger

n. Anger is a feeling of being upset and bad-tempered.

angrily

adv. If you do something *angrily*, you do it in a bad-tempered way.

angry (angrier, angriest)

adj. If you are *angry*, someone or something has made you upset and cross.

animal (animals)

n. All living things except plants, are *animals*.

ankle (ankles)

n. Your *ankle* is the joint between your foot and your leg.

annoy (annoys, annoying, annoyed)

vb. If you *annoy* someone, you do something they don't like and make them cross.

another

If you choose *another* thing, you choose one more than you already have.

answer (answers, answering, answered)

vb. When you *answer* someone, you say something to them in reply to something they have said.

ant (ants)

n. An *ant* is a tiny insect. *Ants* live underground in large groups called colonies.

antelope (antelopes)

n. An *antelope* is an animal that looks like a deer. It has horns and it can run very fast. *Antelopes* live in Africa and Asia.

antenna (antennae)

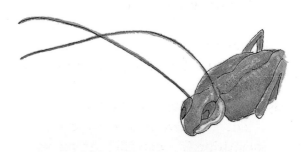

n. Antennae are the long, thin feelers on the head of an insect.

anvil (anvils)

n. An *anvil* is an iron block that blacksmiths use to beat hot metal into shape.

anybody see **anyone**

anyone

When you say *anyone* or *anybody*, you mean any person.

anything

You use the word *anything* to mean no particular thing.

anywhere

adv. Anywhere is in any place.

ape (apes)

n. An *ape* is a large monkey with no tail. Chimpanzees, orang-utans and gibbons are all *apes*.

appear (appears, appearing, appeared)

1. *vb.* If you *appear* from somewhere, you are seen suddenly.
2. *vb.* If someone *appears* on the television, in an advertisement, a play or a film, they take part in it.

appearance (appearances)

n. The *appearance* of someone or something is when they arrive in a place suddenly.

apple (apples)

n. An *apple* is a crisp, round fruit which grows on a tree. It is usually red, yellow or green and it has pips. You can eat it raw or cooked.

apron (aprons)

n. You wear an *apron* to keep the front of your clothes clean when you are cooking or painting.

area (areas)

n. An *area* is a flat part of a space or surface of something.

arm (arms)

1. *n.* Your *arm* is the part of your body which is joined to your shoulder.
2. *n. Arms* are weapons.

armour

n. Armour is special clothing, usually made of metal, that is worn for protection.

army (armies)

n. An *army* is a large group of people who are trained to fight in a war.

around

1. If you look *around* for something, you look all about for it.
2. If you say something is *around*, it is on all sides.

arrange (arranges, arranging, arranged)

1. *vb.* If you *arrange* something, you make plans to do it.
2. *vb.* When you *arrange* objects, you put them in a particular order or position.

arrangement (arrangements)

1. *n.* An *arrangement* of flowers or objects is the way you display them.
2. *n.* If you make an *arrangement* with someone, you say that you will do something for them.

arrival

n. Your *arrival* is the moment that you get there.

arrive (arrives, arriving, arrived)

vb. If you *arrive* somewhere, you get there.

arrow (arrows)

n. An *arrow* is a long, thin weapon with a point at one end. An arrow is shot from a bow.

articulated

adj. An *articulated* vehicle is usually a very long lorry. It is made in two sections joined by a metal bar so that it can turn corners easily.

ash (ashes)

n. *Ash* is the powdery flakes and dust that is left when a fire has finished burning.

ashamed

adj. If you are *ashamed*, you feel very bad about something that you have done.

ashore

adv. If you go *ashore*, you go onto land after being in or on the water.

ask (asks, asking, asked)

vb. If you *ask* someone something, you want to know the answer to a question.

asleep

adj. If you are *asleep*, your eyes are closed and you are not awake.

assistant (assistants)

n. An *assistant* is someone who helps other people to do something.

ate see **eat**

attach (attaches, attaching, attached)
vb. If you *attach* two things, you join them together.

attack (attacks, attacking, attacked)
vb. If one person *attacks* another, they start a fight.

attract (attracts, attracting, attracted)
1. *vb.* If something *attracts* people or animals, there is something about it that makes them want to come to it.
2. *vb.* If a magnet *attracts* pieces of metal, it pulls them towards it.

aunt (aunts)
n. Your *aunt* is your mother or father's sister. You might call her *auntie* or *aunty*.

avalanche (avalanches)

n. An *avalanche* is a huge amount of snow and ice that falls down the side of a mountain.

avenue (avenues)

n. An *avenue* is a wide road, usually with trees on both sides.

avoid (avoids, avoiding, avoided)
vb. If you *avoid* someone or something, you keep away from them.

awake (awakes, awaking, awoke, awoken)
vb. When you are *awake*, your eyes are open and you know what is going on around you.

away
1. *adv.* If something happens *away*, it does not happen here.
2. *adv.* If you tidy something *away*, you put it in another place.

awful
adj. If something is *awful*, it is very bad, ugly or nasty.

baboon (baboons)

n. A *baboon* is a large monkey.

baby (babies)

n. A *baby* is a child or animal that has just been born.

back (backs, backing, backed)

1. *n.* The *back* of something is behind not in front.
2. If you come *back* or get back from somewhere, you return to the place where you began.
3. If you put something *back*, you put it in the place where you found it.

bacon

n. *Bacon* is salty meat from a pig.

bad (worse, worst)

1. *adj.* Food that has gone *bad* is not suitable to eat.
2. *adv.* If you are *bad* you are naughty.

badger (badgers)

n. A *badger* is a large grey animal with black stripes on its face. It lives in a burrow called a sett.

badly

adv. If you do something *badly*, you do not do it as well as you could.

bag (bags)

n. A *bag* holds or carries things. It is open at the top and can be made of paper, leather, cloth or plastic.

bake (bakes, baking, baked)

vb. If you *bake* something, you cook it in an oven.

baker (bakers)

n. A *baker's* job is to work in a bakery, making bread and cakes to sell.

balance (balances, balancing, balanced)

1. *n.* A *balance* is a pair of scales that you use for weighing things.
2. *vb.* If you *balance* on something, you try to keep steady.

ball (balls)

n. A *ball* is a round object that you use for games. It can be soft or hard, large or small.

balloon (balloons)

n. A *balloon* is a small, brightly coloured bag of thin rubber that you can blow up.

banana (bananas)

n. A *banana* is a long, thin, curved fruit with a thick yellow skin.

band (bands)

1. *n.* A *band* is a group of people who play music together to listen to, or to dance to.
2. *n.* A *band* of people or animals is a group that travels about together.
3. *n.* A *band* is a narrow strip of cloth or other material that goes around something.

bandage (bandages, bandaging, bandaged)

1. *n.* A *bandage* is a strip of material that you wrap around a wound.
2. *vb.* If you *bandage* a wound, you wind a strip of material around it to cover it.

bang (bangs, banging, banged)

1. *n.* A *bang* is a sudden loud explosion or noise.
2. *vb.* If two things *bang* together, they hit each other hard.

banish (banishes, banishing, banished)

vb. If you *banish* someone, you send them far away from the country where they live to punish them.

bank (banks)

1. *n.* A *bank* is a place that looks after money and valuable things for people.
2. *n.* A *bank* is the ground on either side of a river.

banner (banners)

> *n.* A *banner* is a large flag that is carried in a procession.

bar (bars)

> *n.* A *bar* is a long, solid piece of wood, metal or chocolate.

bare (barer, barest)

> 1. *adj.* If a person has no clothes on, they are *bare.*
> 2. *adj.* If a cupboard is *bare,* it is empty

barge (barges)

> *n.* A *barge* is a large flat-bottomed boat that is used on canals.

bark (barks, barking, barked)

> 1. *n. Bark* is the tough material that covers the outside of a tree.
> 2. *vb.* When a dog *barks,* it makes a short, loud sound.

barn (barns)

> *n.* A *barn* is a large building on a farm where things can be stored.

barnacle (barnacles)

> *n.* A *barnacle* is a shellfish that clings to rocks and to the bottom of ships.

barrel (barrels)

> *n.* A *barrel* is a round, wooden, metal or plastic container with flat ends. *Barrels* are used for storing liquids.

barrier (barriers)

> *n.* A *barrier* is a fence or an obstacle that is in the way.

base (bases)

> *n.* The *base* is the bottom of something.

bash (bashes, bashing, bashed)

> *vb.* If you *bash* something, you hit it very hard.

basket (baskets)

> *n.* A *basket* is a bag made of canes or thin strips of wood. It is open at the top and has a handle.

bat (bats, batting, batted)

> 1. *n.* A *bat* is a small animal, like a mouse with wings.
> 2. *n.* A *bat* is a piece of wood you use for hitting a ball in a game.
> 3. *vb.* If you *bat* in a game of cricket, you take your turn at hitting the ball.

a **b** c d e f g h i j k l m

bath (baths, bathing, bathed)

1. *n.* A *bath* is a large container that you fill with water and sit or lie in in to wash.
2. *vb.* When you *bath*, you get into a bath to wash.

bathroom (bathrooms)

n. A *bathroom* is a room that contains a bath or a shower, a wash basin and sometimes a toilet.

batter (batters, battering, battered)

1. *n. Batter* is a thick liquid made of flour, eggs and milk, used to make pancakes.
2. *vb.* If you *batter* something, you hit it many times.

battle (battles)

n. A *battle* is a fight in a war between ships, armies or aeroplanes.

bawl (bawls, bawling, bawled)

vb. If you *bawl*, you shout or cry loudly with your mouth wide open.

bazaar (bazaars)

n. A *bazaar* is a large market or a sale of things to raise money for a charity.

beach (beaches)

n. A *beach* is a long stretch of sand or pebbles beside the sea or a lake.

beak (beaks)

n. A *beak* is the hard, pointed or curved part of a bird's mouth.

beam (beams, beaming, beamed)

n. 1. A *beam* is a wide, strong piece of wood used to hold up a roof.
2. *vb.* If you *beam*, you give a huge smile.

bean (beans)

n. A *bean* is a vegetable that grows inside long pods. Broad *beans*, runner beans and kidney beans are all types of bean.

bear (bears, bearing, bore, born)

1. *n.* A *bear* is a large, strong, wild animal with thick fur and sharp claws. *Bears* live in cool countries and some can be very dangerous.
2. *n.* A *bear* is a soft toy usually called a teddy bear.
3. *vb.* When an animal *bears* young, it has babies.

beard (beards)

n. A *beard* is the hair that grows on a man's face.

beast (beasts)

n. A *beast* is a wild animal.

beat (beats, beating, beaten)

1. *vb.* If you *beat* someone in a race or in a competition, you win.
2. *vb.* If you *beat* someone, you hit them again and again, usually with a stick.

beautiful

adj. A *beautiful* person or thing is very pretty or attractive.

beauty (beauties)

n. Beauty is being very attractive to look at.

beaver (beavers)

n. A *beaver* is a brown furry animal with a flat, scaly tail and webbed back feet. *Beavers* build their homes from sticks and mud. A beaver's home is called a lodge.

because

If you say *'because'* you give the reason why.

bed (beds)

n. A *bed* is a piece of furniture to sleep on. It is usually kept in the bedroom.

bedclothes

n. Bedclothes are the duvet or blankets and sheets that you have on your bed.

bedroom (bedrooms)

n. Your *bedroom* is the room where you sleep.

bedtime

n. Bedtime is the time when you usually go to bed at night.

bee (bees)

n. A *bee* is a small flying insect. It has black and yellow stripes and can make honey. Honey *bees* live in a beehive.

beetle (beetles)

n. A *beetle* is an insect with four wings. The outer wings have hard covers that cover the body when the beetle is not flying.

before

Something that happens *before* something else, happens first.

beg (begs, begging, begged)

vb. If a person or animal *begs*, they ask again and again for something.

beggar (beggars)

n. Beggars are people who are so poor that they ask other people to give food, clothes or money to them, to help them to live.

begin (begins, beginning, began, begun)

vb. When you *begin* something, you start it.

beginner (beginners)

n. A *beginner* is a person who is doing something for the first time.

behave (behaves, behaving, behaved)

vb. The way you *behave* is how you act in front of other people.

behind

If something is *behind* something else, it is at the back of it.

believe (believes, believing, believed)

vb. If you *believe* something, you are sure it is true.

bell (bells)

n. A *bell* is a hollow piece of metal which rings when you strike it. Church *bells* are huge and ring when you pull a long rope. A *bell* on a front or back door rings inside the house when you press a button. This type of bell works by electricity.

bellow (bellows, bellowing, bellowed)

vb. If a bull or other large animal *bellows*, it makes a loud, deep noise.

belly (bellies)

n. Your *belly* is the front part of your body below your chest.

belong (belongs, belonging, belonged)

1. *vb.* If you *belong* to something like a club, you are a member of it.
2. *vb.* If something *belongs* to you, it is yours.

below

If something is *below* something else, it is under it.

belt (belts)

n. A *belt* is a piece of leather or material that you wear around your waist.

bend (bends, bending, bent)

vb. Something that *bends* is not straight. If you *bend* something you make it curved.

beneath

If something is *beneath*, it is underneath.

berry (berries)

n. A *berry* is a small, soft, round fruit that grows on a bush or a tree.

beside

If something is *beside* something else, it is at the side of it.

best see **good**

bet (bets, betting, bet)

1. *vb.* If you make a *bet*, you take a chance that you might win some money on the result of an event such as a race.
2. *vb.* If you *bet* someone can or can't do something, you dare them to do it.

better see **good**

between

If one thing is *between* two other things, it is in the middle of them.

beware

vb. If you tell someone to *beware* of something, you warn them to be careful of it.

beyond

Beyond is on the other side of, or further than, a particular place.

bicycle (bicycles)

n. A *bicycle* has two wheels and two pedals. You move the pedals to make the wheels go round. A bicycle is also called a bike.

big (bigger, biggest)

adj. If something is *big*, it is large.

bike see **bicycle**

bill (bills)

n. A *bill* is a written list of money that you owe for things that you have bought.

bin (bins)

n. A *bin* is a container for rubbish.

bird (birds)

n. A *bird* is a creature with two legs and two wings, which is covered with feathers. Most *birds* can fly. The young are hatched from eggs.

birthday (birthdays)

n. Your *birthday* is the special day that you celebrate every year because it is the day you were born.

biscuit (biscuits)

n. A *biscuit* is a crisp, thin cake. It can be sweet or savoury.

bishop (bishops)

n. A *bishop* is an important person in the church who is in charge of the other priests.

bit (bits)

n. A *bit* is a small piece or amount of something.

bite (bites, biting, bit, bitten)

vb. When you *bite* something, you close your teeth on it to break it.

bitter

adj. Something that is *bitter* has a sharp, unpleasant taste.

bitterly

adj. If you say that it is *bitterly* cold, you mean that it is extremely cold.

black (blacker, blackest)

adj. *Black* is the darkest colour there is. It is the colour of the night sky when there is no light at all.

blackbird (blackbirds)

n. A *blackbird* is a common wild bird. The male has black feathers and a yellow beak, and the female has brown feathers.

blacksmith (blacksmiths)

n. A *blacksmith* is a person whose job it is to make things out of metal, usually horseshoes and other farm tools.

bladder (bladders)

n. A *bladder* is the part of the body that stores waste water.

blanket (blankets)

n. A *blanket* is a large piece of warm cloth, often used as a bed cover.

blew see **blow**

blind

adj. Someone who is *blind* cannot see.

block (blocks)

1. n. A *block* of flats or offices is a tall building where many people live or work.
2. n. A *block* is a large lump shaped like a rectangle.

blood

n. *Blood* is the red liquid that your heart pumps around your body.

blow (blows, blowing, blew, blown)

1. n. A *blow* is a very hard knock.
2. vb. If you *blow*, you make air come out of your mouth.
3. vb. When the wind *blows*, everything is moved about by it.

blubber

n. *Blubber* is the fat of a whale.

blue (bluer, bluest)

adj. Something that is *blue* is the colour of the sky on a summer day.

boa (boas)

1. n. A *boa* is a large snake which crushes its prey.

2. n. A *boa* is a long scarf made of feathers.

boar (boars)

n. A *boar* is a male pig.

board (boards, boarding, boarded)

1. n. A *board* is a thin, flat piece of wood.
2. vb. If you *board* a ship, a train or an aeroplane, you get on it.

boat (boats)

n. A *boat* is a small ship that can take people and goods over water.

a **b** c d e f g h i j k l m

body (bodies)

n. Your *body* is the whole of you.

boil (boils, boiling, boiled)

vb. If you *boil* water, milk or any other liquid, you heat it until it bubbles and steams and is very hot.

boiler (boilers)

n. A *boiler* is a large container in which you heat liquids.

bold (bolder, boldest)

adj. A *bold* person is brave and not afraid.

bomb (bombs)

n. A *bomb* is a weapon that explodes and does a lot of damage.

bone (bones)

n. The hard parts of your body are made of *bone*. All your *bones* together make your skeleton.

bonfire (bonfires)

n. A *bonfire* is a large fire that you burn outdoors.

book (books)

n. A *book* is made of many pages of paper fixed together inside a cover.

boom (booms, booming, boomed)

1. *n.* A *boom* is a very loud, deep noise.
2. *vb.* If something *booms*, it makes a a very loud, deep sound.

boot (boots, booting, booted)

1. *n.* A *boot* covers your foot, ankle and sometimes your leg up to your knee.

2. *n.* The *boot* of a car is the space with no seats where you can put cases, shopping or other large things.
3. *vb.* If you *boot* a ball, you kick it hard.

border (borders)

n. The *border* of something is the edge of it.

bore (bores, boring, bored)

1. *n.* A *bore* is a person who is not interesting.
2. *vb.* If you *bore* people, you make them feel tired and fed up because they are not interested in you.
3. *adj.* If you are *bored,* you feel tired and fed up because you are not interested in doing anything.

born see **bear.**

borrow (borrows, borrowing, borrowed)

vb. If you *borrow* something from someone, they let you have or use it for a while but expect you to give it back.

both

Both means the two of them.

bother (bothers, bothering, bothered)

1. *vb.* If you *bother* about something, you take trouble over it.
2. If you say '*Bother!*', you are cross with yourself because you have done something silly.

bottle (bottles)

n. A *bottle* is a container for storing liquids. It is usually narrow at the top. Some *bottles* are made of glass or plastic and hold cold liquids like milk or juice. Some bottles, like hot water bottles, are specially made of rubber to hold hot liquids.

bottom (bottoms)

n. The *bottom* of something is the lowest part.

bought see **buy**

bounce (bounces, bouncing, bounced)

vb. If you *bounce* a ball, you hit it against something hard and it springs back. Something *bouncy* is springy.

bound (bounds, bounding, bounded)

vb. If a person or an animal *bounds*, it leaps and jumps.

bow (bows) *rhymes with grow*

1. *n.* A *bow* is a knot tied with loops.
2. *n.* A *bow* is a weapon for shooting arrows. It is a long piece of wood bent into a curve by a string joined to each end.

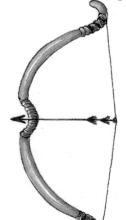

bow (bows, bowing, bowed) *rhymes with cow*

vb. When you *bow*, you bend your body forward for a moment as a way of saying 'hello' to someone.

bowl (bowls)

n. A *bowl* is a round, deep dish for liquid or food.

box (boxes)

n. A *box* is a container with flat or rounded sides. It may have a lid.

boy (boys)

n. A *boy* is a male child.

brake (brakes, braking, braked)

1. n. *Brakes* are the parts of a car or bicycle that make it stop.
2. vb. When a car *brakes*, it stops very quickly.

bramble (brambles)

n. A *bramble* is part of a prickly bush or a blackberry bush.

bran

n. *Bran* is the small brown flakes that are left after the wheat for white flour has been taken out of wheat grains.

branch (branches)

n. A *branch* is a part of a tree that grows out from its trunk like an arm.

brass (brasses)

n. *Brass* is a yellow metal made by mixing copper and other metals.

brawl (brawls, brawling, brawled)

1. n. If there is a *brawl*, many people fight each other with their fists or struggle roughly.
2. vb. If you *brawl*, you fight roughly with several other people.

bray (brays, braying, brayed)

vb. When a donkey *brays*, it makes a long harsh noise.

bread

n. *Bread* is a food made of flour, water and, often, yeast.

break (breaks, breaking, broke, broken)

vb. If you *break* something, it splits into pieces or stops working.

breakfast (breakfasts)

n. *Breakfast* is the meal you eat when you get up in the morning. It is the first meal of the day.

breast (breasts)

n. The *breast* is a person's or animal's chest.

breath (breaths)

n. *Breath* is the air that you take into your body through your nose.

breathe (breathes, breathing, breathed)

vb. When you *breathe*, you take air into your lungs and let it out again.

breed (breeds, breeding, bred)

1. n. The *breed* of an animal is a particular type of animal.
2. vb. If you *breed* animals you keep them to produce young.

breeze (breezes)

n. A *breeze* is a gentle wind.

brewery (breweries)

n. A *brewery* is a place where beer is made. A brewery is also the name of a company that makes beer.

brick (bricks)

n. A *brick* is a rectangular block used for making buildings.

bride (brides)

n. A *bride* is a woman on her wedding day.

bridge (bridges)

n. A *bridge* is a road that is built over rivers, railways and roads so that people and vehicles can cross over in safety.

bright (brighter, brightest)

adj. If something is *bright*, it shines strongly.

brightness

n. The *brightness* of something is how shiny it is.

brilliant

1. adj. A *brilliant* colour is very bright.
2. adj. If you are *brilliant* at something, you are very, very good at it.

bring (brings, bringing, brought)

vb. If you *bring* something to a place, it comes with you when you go there.

broken see **break**

a **b** c d e f g h i j k l m

brood (broods, brooding, brooded)
1. *n.* A *brood* is a family of young birds.
2. *vb.* If someone *broods*, they think about their worries a great deal.

broom (brooms)
n. A *broom* is a type of brush for sweeping the floor.

brother (brothers)
n. Your *brother* is a boy who has the same mother and father as you.

brought see **bring**

brown (browner, brownest)
adj. Something that is *brown* is the colour of the earth or wood.

brush (brushes, brushing, brushed)
1. *n.* A *brush* is an object made of wood, plastic, or metal with bristles fixed to it. There are many different sizes and uses for brushes.
2. *vb.* If you *brush* something such as your hair or an animal's fur, you use a brush to tidy it.

bubble (bubbles, bubbling, bubbled)

1. *n.* A *bubble* is a ball of air inside a thin film of liquid.
2. *vb.* If something *bubbles*, lots of balls of air appear in it.

bucket (buckets)
n. A *bucket* is a container with a handle for carrying water and other things. It has no lid.

bud (buds)

n. A *bud* is a small pointed lump that begins to grow on a plant and turns into a leaf or a flower.

buffalo (buffaloes)
n. A *buffalo* is a large, wild animal like a cow with curved horns and a shaggy coat. There are many different types of buffalo that live in Asia, Africa and America.

build (builds, building, built)

vb. If you *build* something, you join things together to make it. A builder joins bricks together to make a building.

bulge (bulges, bulging, bulged)

1. *n.* A *bulge* is a lump in something that is usually flat.
2. *vb.* If something *bulges*, it swells out.

bull (bulls)

n. A *bull* is a male animal of the cow family.

bump (bumps, bumping, bumped)

1. *n.* A *bump* is a small swelling.
2. *vb.* If you *bump* something, you knock it.

bunch (bunches)

n. A *bunch* is a group of things or people who are alike in some way.

bungalow (bungalows)

n. A *bungalow* is a house built only on one level.

burger (burgers)

n. A *burger* is a bun filled with a flat, round piece of minced beef and, sometimes, onions.

burglar (burglars)

n. A *burglar* is a thief who breaks into houses and steals things.

burn (burns, burning, burned or burnt)

1. *vb.* If you *burn* fuel such as coal or wood, you make a fire.
2. *vb.* If something hot *burns* you, it hurts you with heat.
3. *vb.* An engine *burns* oil to make it work.

burp (burps, burping, burped)

vb. If someone *burps*, they make a noise when air comes up through their throat from their stomach.

burrow (burrows, burrowing, burrowed)

1. *n.* A *burrow* is a long tunnel or hole underground.
2. *vb.* If an animal *burrows*, it digs a tunnel or a hole under the ground.

burst (bursts, bursting, burst)

vb. If something *bursts*, it breaks open and everything that was inside falls out.

bury (buries, burying, buried)
vb. If you *bury* something, you dig a hole, put it into the ground and cover it over again with earth.

bus (buses)

n. A *bus* is a large vehicle for taking many people from one place to another.

bush (bushes)
n. A *bush* is a large woody plant with lots of branches.

busy (busier, busiest)
adj. A *busy* person works hard at something and has very little time to do anything else.

butcher (butchers)

n. A *butcher* is a person who cuts up and sells meat and poultry in a shop.

butter
n. Butter is a solid, yellow fat made from cream that you can spread on bread.

butterfly (butterflies)
n. A *butterfly* is an insect with four large wings. It begins life as an egg, hatches out into a caterpillar, then spins a cocoon around itself and later comes out as a butterfly.

button (buttons)
n. A *button* is small and round with holes in the middle so it can be sewn onto cloth. Buttons are used to hold clothes together and they are usually made of plastic or wood.

buy (buys, buying, bought)
vb. If you *buy* something, you pay money to get it.

buzz (buzzes, buzzing, buzzed)
vb. If something *buzzes*, it makes a noise that sounds like a bee.

cabbage (cabbages)
n. A *cabbage* is a round, leafy vegetable. It is usually green but it can also be red or white.

café (cafés)

n. A *café* is a place where you can get a cup of tea or coffee and snacks.

cake (cakes)
n. A *cake* is a sweet food usually made from eggs, flour, sugar and margarine and baked in an oven.

calendar (calendars)
n. A *calendar* is a list which shows all the days of the week and the months of the year.

call (calls, calling, called)
1. *vb.* If you *call*, you speak loudly.
2. *vb.* If you *call* someone something, you give them a name.
3. *vb.* If you *call* someone, you tell them to come to you.

camel (camels)
n. A *camel* is a large animal with one or two humps on its back. *Camels* are used instead of horses in deserts as they can travel a long way without eating or drinking.

camp (camps, camping, camped)

1. *n.* A *camp* is a place where people stop for a short time. They may use tents or caravans for shelter.
2. *vb.* If you *camp*, you stay in a tent overnight or for a holiday.

a b **c** d e f g h i j k l m

canal (canals)

n. A *canal* is a man-made river. It is usually straight.

candle (candles)

n. A *candle* is a stick of wax with a piece of string, called a wick, through the middle. *Candles* give light as they burn.

cape (capes)

n. A *cape* is a short cloak.

caper (capers, capering, capered)

vb. If you *caper*, you dance and leap about in a lively way.

captain (captains)

n. A *captain* is an important officer in the army or the navy.

car (cars)

n. A *car* is a machine with four wheels and an engine that carries passengers by road.

cardboard

n. Very thick, strong paper is called *cardboard*. It is used to make things like boxes.

cardigan (cardigans)

n. A *cardigan* is a knitted jacket that has buttons.

care (cares, caring, cared)

1. *vb.* If you *care* about someone or something, they are important to you and you like them.
2. If you take *care* of someone or something, you look after them.
3. If you say 'Take *care*', you tell someone to look after himself or herself.

careful

adj. A *careful* person makes sure that they do things in a sensible way without damaging anything or making a mistake.

carefully

adv. If you do something *carefully*, you do it so that you do not hurt anything.

n o p q r s t u v w x y z   **29**

caretaker (caretakers)

n. A *caretaker* looks after a building as a job.

carpet (carpets)

n. A *carpet* is a floor covering which is usually made of something like wool.

carriage (carriages)

1. *n.* A *carriage* is the part of a train where passengers travel.
2. *n.* A *carriage* is a horse-drawn vehicle with four wheels.

carry (carries, carrying, carried)

vb. If you *carry* something, you lift it up and take it from one place to another.

cart (carts)

n. A *cart* is a small vehicle on wheels that you can pull or push. Sometimes horses or cattle pull *carts*, especially on farms.

case (cases)

n. A *case* is a box with a handle that you can put your clothes in to go on holiday.

cast (casts, casting, cast)

1. *n.* The *cast* of a play or a film is all the people who act in it.

2. *vb.* When a fisherman *casts* a line, he throws the end with bait on it into the water.

castle (castles)

n. A *castle* is a very big, old building with very thick walls. *Castles* were built many years ago to protect the people living inside from their enemies.

cat (cats)

n. A *cat* is a mammal. Often small *cats* are kept as pets. Larger cats, like lions and tigers, live in the wild.

a b **c** d e f g h i j k l m

catch (catches, catching, caught)

1. *n.* A *catch* in a game like cricket is when you catch the ball after the batsman has hit it, but before it touches the ground.

2. *vb.* If you *catch* something like a ball, you take hold of it when it comes towards you through the air.
3. *vb.* If you *catch* an animal, you trap it.
4. *vb.* If the police *catch* criminals, they take them to the police station.
5. *vb.* If you *catch* a cold, you sneeze, your nose runs and you feel ill.
6. *vb.* If you *catch* a train, you get on it to go somewhere.

caterpillar (caterpillars)

n. A *caterpillar* is a small creature like a worm with legs. It can be many different colours. *Caterpillars* grow into butterflies or moths.

cattle

n. Cattle are cows and bulls which are usually kept on a farm.

caught see **catch**

cause (causes, causing, caused)

1. *n.* A *cause* is a reason for doing something. Charities raise money for good *causes*.
2. *vb.* If you *cause* something to happen, you make it happen.

cave (caves)

n. A *cave* is a large underground hole in a cliff or hillside.

cell (cells)

1. *n.* A *cell* is a small room where prisoners are kept.
2. *n.* A *cell* is the tiniest part of any living thing that can live on its own.
3. *n.* A *cell* is a hole in a honeycomb where the queen bee lays her eggs.

centimetre (centimetres)

n. A *centimetre* is a measurement of length. It is the same as 10 millimetres.

centipede (centipedes)

n. A *centipede* is a small, thin creature that looks like a worm but has many small legs.

centre (centres)

1. *n.* The *centre* of something is the middle of it.

I'm in the centre

2. *n.* A *centre* for something is the main place where things like shopping or sport happen.

century (centuries)

n. A *century* is one hundred years.

cereal (cereals)

1. *n.* A *cereal* is any plant that farmers grow for grain. Oats, barley and wheat are *cereals*.

2. *n.* *Cereal* is a food made from the seed of cereal plants that you eat for breakfast.

ceremony (ceremonies)

n. A *ceremony* is a special and important occasion, when a group of people gather together to watch or take part in it.

certain

adj. If you are *certain* about something, you are sure about it.

chain (chains)

n. A *chain* is a string of metal links fixed together.

chair (chairs)

n. A *chair* is a seat for one person.

chamber (chambers)

n. A *chamber* is an old-fashioned word for a room.

champion (champions)

n. The *champion* is the winner of a competition. Champ is short for champion.

change (changes, changing, changed)

vb. When something *changes*, it becomes different.

channel (channels)

n. A *channel* is a narrow stretch of water between two pieces of land.

chaos

n. If there is *chaos*, there is complete muddle and everything gets mixed up.

a b **c** d e f g h i j k l m

chapter (chapters)

n. A *chapter* is a section of a book.

charge (charges, charging, charged)

1. *n.* A *charge* is a sudden attack.
2. *n.* A *charge* is the price you have to pay for something.
3. *vb.* If a bull *charges*, it rushes towards you as if it will not stop.

chariot (chariots)

n. A *chariot* is a small cart with two wheels pulled by horses. Long ago, *chariots* were used for fighting and racing contests.

charming

adj. A *charming* person is attractive and pleasant to be with.

chase (chases, chasing, chased)

vb. If you *chase* someone or something, you run after them and try to catch them.

chat (chats, chatting, chatted)

1. *n.* A *chat* is a friendly talk with someone.
2. *vb.* If you *chat* with someone, you talk about things that are not very important in a friendly way.

chatter (chatters, chattering, chattered)

1. *vb.* When people *chatter*, they talk a lot and very quickly.
2. *vb.* If your teeth *chatter*, they make a rattling noise.

check (checks, checking, checked)

1. *n.* *Check* is a pattern made of squares.
2. *vb.* If you *check* something, you look at it carefully to see if it is alright.

cheek (cheeks)

n. Your *cheeks* are the sides of your face below your eyes.

cheep (cheeps, cheeping, cheeped)

vb. If a baby bird *cheeps*, it makes a little squeaking sound.

cheer (cheers, cheering, cheered)

1. *n.* A *cheer* is a loud shout from a crowd who want their team to win.

2. *vb.* If you *cheer,* you shout loudly and joyfully to show you are pleased or to encourage someone.

cheese (cheeses)

n. Cheese is a food made from milk which has been stirred until it is thick. Then the liquid is squeezed out of it and the solid part left behind is called cheese.

cheetah (cheetahs)

n. A *cheetah* is a large, wild member of the cat family. *Cheetahs* can run very fast.

cherry (cherries)

n. A *cherry* is a small, round, soft fruit. *Cherries* are red or black.

chest (chests)

1. *n.* A *chest* is a large, strong box.
2. *n.* Your *chest* is the upper part of your body, between your neck and your waist.

chest of drawers (chests of drawers)

n. A *chest of drawers* is a piece of furniture used for storing clothes.

chestnut (chestnuts)

n. Chestnuts are the fruit of the *chestnut* tree. They are shiny, reddish-brown nuts in spiky green cases. Chestnuts can be roasted and eaten.

chew (chews, chewing, chewed)

vb. When you *chew* your food, you crush it with your teeth by moving your jaw.

chick (chicks)

n. A *chick* is a baby bird.

chicken (chickens)

n. A *chicken* is a bird which is kept on a farm for its eggs and its meat.

chief (chiefs)

n. The *chief* is the leader or head of something.

child (children)

n. A *child* is a young boy or girl.

chill (chills, chilling, chilled)

1. *n.* If you have a *chill,* you are cold and shivery and not very well.
2. *vb.* If you *chill* something, you make it cold.

chilly (chillier, chilliest)

adj. If the weather is *chilly,* it is cold.

chime (chimes, chiming, chimed)
vb. When a bell *chimes*, it rings.

chimney (chimneys)
n. A *chimney* is a tall pipe that goes from a fireplace, or a factory furnace, up above the roof of the building. It takes the smoke away into the air.

chimpanzee (chimpanzees)
n. A *chimpanzee* is a large ape with a short tail. *Chimpanzees* come from Africa.

chin (chins)
n. Your *chin* is the part of your face below your mouth.

china
n. *China* is very fine and delicate pottery.

chip (chips, chipping, chipped)
1. *n.* A *chip* is a small piece of something.
2. *n.* *Chips* are small pieces of potato cut into strips and fried.
3. *vb.* If you *chip* something, you break a small piece off.

chocolate (chocolates)
n. *Chocolate* is a hard, brown sweet made from cocoa, milk and sugar.

choose (chooses, choosing, chose, chosen)
vb. If you *choose* something, you pick out the one you want. You make a *choice*.

chop (chops)

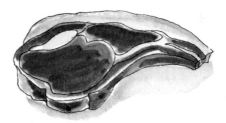

n. A *chop* is a small, thick piece of meat on a bone.

chorus (choruses)

1. *n.* A *chorus* is a group of people who sing together.
2. *n.* A *chorus* is a verse that you sing over and over again in a song.

chose see **choose**

christening (christenings)

n. A *christening* is a Christian service in church when a baby is given its name.

Christmas

n. Christmas is the time of year when Jesus Christ's birthday is celebrated. Christmas Day is on 25th December.

chrysalis (chrysalises)

n. A *chrysalis* is the cocoon of a butterfly or moth when it is no longer a larva but not yet an adult. A chrysalis has a hard outside shell.

chuckle (chuckles, chuckling, chuckled)

vb. If you *chuckle,* you give a low, giggly laugh.

church (churches)

n. A *church* is a building where people worship God.

circle (circles, circling, circled)

1. *n.* A *circle* is a curved line with both ends joined. It makes the shape of a ring.

2. *vb.* If you *circle* a place, you go around the outside of it.

circus (circuses)

n. A *circus* is a show held in a tent called a Big Top. Acrobats, clowns and jugglers all perform tricks to entertain the people who come to watch.

city (cities)

n. A *city* is a very big and busy town.

claim (claims, claiming, claimed)

vb. If you *claim* something, you say that it belongs to you.

clan (clans)

n. A *clan* is a large family. Clans are usually found in Scotland.

clang (clangs, clanging, clanged)

vb. If something *clangs,* it makes a noisy, ringing sound.

a b **c** d e f g h i j k l m

clank (clanks, clanking, clanked)
vb. If something *clanks*, it sounds like big pieces of metal banging together.

clap (claps, clapping, clapped)
vb. When you *clap* your hands, you make a noise by hitting your hands together.

class (classes)

n. A *class* is a group of children who have lessons together in school.

clatter (clatters, clattering, clattered)
1. *n.* If you make a *clatter,* you make short, loud noises one after the other.
2. *vb.* You *clatter* when you hit hard things together very quickly and loudly.

claw (claws, clawing, clawed)
1. *n.* A *claw* is a hard, sharp nail on an animal's foot.
2. *vb.* If you *claw* at something, you scratch or tear at it.

clean (cleans, cleaning, cleaned; cleaner, cleanest)
1. *vb.* If you *clean* something, you take away the dirt.
2. *adj.* A *clean* person, animal or place is tidy and not dirty.

clear (clears, clearing, cleared)
vb. If you *clear* things away, you tidy up.

clever (cleverer, cleverest)
adj. A *clever* person or animal is able to learn quickly and do many things.

cliff (cliffs)
n. A *cliff* is a steep rock face on the side of a hill.

climb (climbs, climbing, climbed)
vb. If you *climb* a hill or a ladder, you go up it.

climber (climbers)
n. A *climber* climbs up mountains or rocks.

cling (clings, clinging, clung)

vb. If you *cling* to something, you hold onto it very tightly.

clinic (clinics)

n. A *clinic* is a kind of hospital where people go to get advice about their health.

cloak (cloaks)

n. A *cloak* is a long coat with no sleeves.

clock (clocks)

n. A *clock* is a machine that measures time.

close (closes, closing, closed; closer, closest)

1. *vb.* When you *close* a door, you shut it.
2. *adj.* If you are *close* to something, you are near to it.

cloth (cloths)

n. A *cloth* is a piece of fabric that you use to clean things.

clothes

n. *Clothes* are things you wear to cover your body.

cloud (clouds)

n. A *cloud* is a patch of white or grey that floats in the sky. *Clouds* are made of many tiny drops of water which sometimes fall as rain.

cloudburst (cloudbursts)

n. A *cloudburst* is a sudden and heavy downpour of rain.

clover (clovers)

n. *Clover* is a small, pink, wild flower that grows in grass.

clown (clowns)

n. A *clown* works in a circus and wears funny clothes. *Clowns* paint their faces and do silly things to make you laugh.

cluck (clucks, clucking, clucked)

vb. If you *cluck,* you make a noise like a hen.

a b **c** d e f g h i j k l m

clung see **cling**

clue (clues)

n. A *clue* is something that helps you to find the answer to a puzzle.

clutch (clutches, clutching, clutched)

1. *n.* The *clutch* is one of the controls in a car.
2. *vb.* If you *clutch* something, you hold it tightly.

coach (coaches, coaching, coached)

1. *n.* A *coach* is a motor vehicle with wheels and an engine that carries many people on journeys.
2. *n.* A *coach* is a carriage pulled by horses.
3. *adj.* A *coaching* inn was a place where people used to stop for refreshment.

coal

n. *Coal* is hard, black rock that is dug out from under the ground. It is burned to give heat.

coast (coasts)

n. The *coast* of a country is the land next to the sea.

coat (coats)

n. A *coat* is a piece of clothing with long sleeves that you wear over the top of your other clothes.

coat-of-arms (coats-of-arms)

A *coat-of-arms* is a special design that belongs to a family, a town or city, or to a particular group of people. *Coats-of-arms* are usually found on shields.

cobweb (cobwebs)

n. A *cobweb* is a fine net that a spider builds to catch its prey.

cockatoo (cockatoos)

n. A *cockatoo* is a parrot that comes from Australia. It has a crest on its head.

cockchafer (cockchafers)

n. A *cockchafer* is a large beetle.

cockle (cockles)

n. *Cockles* are small shellfish that you can eat.

cockroach (cockroaches)

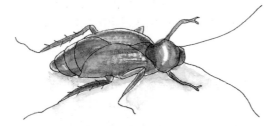

n. A *cockroach* is a beetle that likes dark and dirty places.

cocoa

n. *Cocoa* is a hot chocolate drink.

coconut (coconuts)

n. A *coconut* is a large fruit with a hard shell. Inside there is a sweet, milky liquid and white flesh that you can eat.

cocoon (cocoons)

n. A *cocoon* is a silky case that some insects build to protect themselves while they develop.

coffee

n. Coffee is a hot drink that is made from coffee beans.

coin (coins)

n. A coin is a piece of metal money.

colander (colanders)

n. A *colander* is a bowl with holes in it that you use to wash or drain water from food.

cold (colder, coldest)

1. *adj.* If the weather is *cold*, the temperature outside is low.
2. *adj.* If something is *cold*, it is not hot or warm.

collect (collects, collecting, collected)

vb. If you *collect* something, you go and fetch it from another place. Some people collect things as their job.

collection (collections)

n. A *collection* is a set of things that have been gathered together in one place.

collector (collectors)

n. A *collector* keeps special things like stamps, thimbles, model cars and books.

colony (colonies)

n. A *colony* is a group of people, animals or insects that live together.

a b **c** d e f g h i j k l m

colour (colours, colouring, coloured)

1. *n.* Red, blue and green are *colours*.
2. *vb.* If you *colour* something, you use crayons or paints on it.
3. *adj.* If something is *coloured*, it is a particular colour.

comb (combs, combing, combed)
n. A *comb* is a strip of metal, plastic or wood with a row of thin teeth. You use a comb to tidy your hair.

comic (comics)
1. *n.* A *comic* is a magazine with stories told in pictures.
2. *n.* A *comic* is an entertainer who tells jokes.
3. *adj.* Something *comic* amuses you and makes you want to laugh.

command (commands, commanding, commanded)
1. *n.* A *command* is an order.
2. *vb.* If you *command* someone to do something, you tell them to do it and expect them to obey you.

common (commons)
n. A *common* is a piece of land that belongs to the people who live nearby. It can be used as a meeting place or for keeping animals.

commotion (commotions)
n. A *commotion* is a great deal of noise.

community (communities)
n. A *community* in an area, town or village is the group of people who live there.

competition (competitions)
n. A *competition* is an event where people try to find out who is the best.

complete (completes, completing, completed)
vb. If you *complete* something, you finish it.

compost (composts)
n. *Compost* is the waste from the garden that rots down and can be used to help everything else in the garden to grow.

computer (computers)

n. A *computer* is a machine which stores information and works out problems.

condition (conditions)

n. The *condition* of something is the way it is.

conditioner (conditioners)

n. A *conditioner* is a cream or liquid that makes your hair soft.

cone (cones)

n. A *cone* is a solid shape with a point at the top and a circular base.

conker (conkers)

n. A *conker* is the dried, round fruit of a horse-chestnut tree.

contain (contains, containing, contained)

vb. If a box or a bag *contains* something, there is something inside it.

contents

n. The *contents* of something, like a box or a bag, is what is inside it.

continue (continues, continuing, continued)

vb. If you *continue* to do something, you go on doing it.

contrary

adj. A *contrary* person is bad tempered. They do everything they should not do and annoy other people.

control (controls, controlling, controlled)

vb. If you *control* something, you are in charge of it and make it do what you want.

cook (cooks, cooking, cooked)

1. *n.* A *cook* is a person who cooks food for other people.
2. *vb.* If you *cook* food, you heat it before you eat it. Boiling, frying, baking, roasting, grilling and steaming are all ways of *cooking* food.

cool (cooler, coolest)

adj. If something is *cool*, it is not hot or cold.

copper

n. *Copper* is a reddish-brown metal.

corn

n. *Corn* is the name for cereal crops like wheat and barley.

a b **c** d e f g h i j k l m

corner (corners)

n. A *corner* is the place where two edges, two streets or two walls meet.

cornflakes

n. Cornflakes are a breakfast cereal that you eat with milk and, sometimes, sugar.

coronation (coronations)

n. A *coronation* is the crowning of a new king or queen.

corridor (corridors)

n. A *corridor* is a long passageway in a building.

cosy (cosier, cosiest)

adj. A *cosy* place is warm and comfortable.

cottage (cottages)

n. A *cottage* is a small house, usually in the country.

cotton (cottons)

1. *n. Cotton* is a thread used for sewing.
2. *n. Cotton* is a light material used for making clothes.
3. *n. Cotton* is a plant that is grown in hot countries. The soft fibres around its seeds are used to make thread and material.

count (counts, counting, counted)

1. *vb.* When you *count*, you say numbers in order: one, two, three...
2. *vb.* If you *count* people, animals or objects, you add them up to see how many there are.

country (countries)

1. *n.* The *country* is a place away from towns where there are fields, woods and rivers. It is also called the countryside.
2. *n.* A *country* is a place which has its own people and laws.

county (counties)

n. A *county* is a large area of a country which has its own local government.

couple (couples)

n. A *couple* is two of something. Sometimes two people who are married are called a couple.

course (courses)

n. The *course* of something is the way it goes. The course of a river is the path it takes. A race course is the place where races are held.

cousin (cousins)

n. Your *cousin* is the child of your aunt or uncle.

cover (covers, covering, covered)

vb. If you *cover* something, you put something over it to protect it or to hide it.

cow (cows)

n. A *cow* is a large farm animal that gives milk.

cowboy (cowboys)

n. In America, a *cowboy* rides on a horse to look after a large herd of cattle.

crab (crabs)

n. A *crab* is a sea animal with a hard shell, two large claws and eight legs.

crack (cracks, cracking, cracked)

1. *n.* A *crack* is a thin opening where something has been partly broken.
2. *vb.* If you *crack* something, you tap it and break it open.
3. *vb.* If something *cracks*, it breaks without falling apart completely.

cradle (cradles)

n. A *cradle* is a small bed for a baby.

crane (cranes)

n. A *crane* is a machine that moves very heavy things.

crash (crashes, crashing, crashed)

1. *n.* A *crash* is a sudden, loud, breaking sound.
2. *vb.* If you *crash* around, you make a lot of noise as you move.

crawl (crawls, crawling, crawled)

vb. If you *crawl*, you move along on your hands and knees.

crayon (crayons)

n. A *crayon* is a wax stick or a coloured pencil.

crazy (crazier, craziest)

adj. If you do something *crazy*, you do something in a strange, silly or foolish way.

cream

n. *Cream* is the thick, fatty layer on top of milk.

creamy (creamier, creamiest)

adj. If something is *creamy*, it is thick and smooth to touch or taste.

creep (creeps, creeping, crept)

vb. If you *creep*, you move slowly and quietly.

creepy (creepier, creepiest)

adj. If you are in a *creepy* place, you feel a little scared.

cress

n. *Cress* is a small salad plant.

cricket

n. *Cricket* is a game played by two teams in a field. They use a ball, two bats and two wickets.

crinkly (crinklier, crinkliest)

adj. If something is *crinkly*, it is wrinkled and dry.

crisp (crisps; crisper, crispest)

1. *n.* *Crisps* are thin slices of deep-fried potato.
2. *adj.* If something is *crisp*, it is hard and dry and easy to break.

crocodile (crocodiles)

n. A *crocodile* is a large reptile that lives in rivers and swamps in Africa, India and Australia.

crop (crops)

n. *Crops* are plants such as corn or vegetables that are grown on farms for food.

cross (crosses, crossing, crossed)

    1. *n.* A *cross* is a monument. It could be a special sign to remember people who gave their lives for their country in a war.

    2. *vb.* If you *cross* something like a road, you go from one side to another.

crossly

    adv. If you say something *crossly,* you sound bad-tempered.

crouch (crouches, crouching, crouched)

    vb. When you *crouch,* you bend your knees and get close to the ground without actually sitting down.

crowd (crowds)

    n. A *crowd* is a large number of people gathered together.

crown (crowns, crowning, crowned)

    1. *n.* A *crown* is the ring of silver or gold that a king or queen wears on their head.

    2. *vb.* If someone is *crowned,* they are made king or queen.

crunch (crunches, crunching, crunched)

    vb. If you *crunch* something hard, you crush it noisily between your back teeth.

crush (crushes, crushing, crushed)

    vb. If you *crush* something, you press it very hard until it changes shape or breaks.

crust (crusts)

    n. A *crust* is the hard, crispy outside part of bread or puddings which have been baked in the oven.

cry (cries, crying, cried)

    vb. If you *cry,* you are sad and tears fall from your eyes.

cub (cubs)

    n. A *cub* is a baby fox or lion.

cuddle (cuddles, cuddling, cuddled)

vb. If you *cuddle* someone, you put your arms around them and hold them.

cup (cups)

n. A *cup* is a small container with a handle which is used for drinking liquids.

cupboard (cupboards)

n. A *cupboard* is a piece of furniture or a space inside a wall with shelves and space for storing things.

cure (cures, curing, cured)

vb. If doctors *cure* someone who is sick, they make them well.

curl (curls, curling, curled)

1. *n.* A *curl* is a twist of hair.
2. *vb.* If a person or animal *curls* up, they make themselves into a little ball.

curly (curlier, curliest)

adj. *Curly* hair has many twists and waves in it.

currant (currants)

n. A *currant* is a dried grape. *Currants* are used for cooking.

curtain (curtains)

n. A *curtain* is a covering for a window. It is made of gathered material and hangs from a rail.

curve (curves, curving, curved)

1. *n.* A *curve* is a line which bends round.
2. *vb.* If a road *curves*, it does not go in a straight line.

customer (customers)

n. A *customer* is a person who uses a shop or a bank.

cut (cuts, cutting, cut)

vb. If you *cut* something, you use something sharp like a knife or a pair of scissors to divide it.

cycle (cycles, cycling, cycled)

1. *n.* A *cycle* is a name for a bicycle.
2. *vb.* If you *cycle,* you ride on a bicycle.

cyclist (cyclists)

n. A *cyclist* is a person who rides a bicycle.

cyclone (cyclones)

n. A *cyclone* is a very strong wind which blows in a spiral like a corkscrew.

cygnet (cygnets)

n. A *cygnet* is a baby swan.

cylinder (cylinders)

n. A *cylinder* is a shape like a tube.

dabble (dabbles, dabbling, dabbled)

vb. If you *dabble* your fingers or toes in water, you put them into it and move them about.

dad (dads)

n. Dad and daddy are family names for father.

daft (dafter, daftest)

adj. If you are *daft,* you are funny and foolish.

daily

adv. If you do something *daily,* you do it each day.

daisy (daisies)

n. A *daisy* is a small, white flower with a yellow centre that grows in short grass.

dam (dams, damming, dammed)

1. *n.* A *dam* is a wall that is built to hold back water.
2. *vb.* If you *dam* a river, you make a wall across it to stop the water flowing and to make a lake.

damage (damages, damaging, damaged)

vb. If you *damage* something, you harm or spoil it.

damp (damper, dampest)

adj. If something is *damp,* it is slightly wet.

dance (dances, dancing, danced)

1. *n.* A *dance* is a series of movements to music.

2. *vb.* When you *dance,* you move about in time to music.

danger (dangers)

n. Danger is something that might hurt or harm you.

dangerous

adj. If something is *dangerous*, it is able to hurt or harm you.

dare (dares, daring, dared)

vb. If you *dare* to do something, you are brave or cheeky enough to do it.

dark (darker, darkest)

adj. If it is *dark*, there is no light.

daughter (daughters)

n. A *daughter* is someone's female child.

dawn (dawns, dawning, dawned)

n. Dawn is the first light of the day. It is the time when the sun rises.

day (days)

n. Day is when it is light and you can see. It begins when the sun comes up and ends when the sun goes down. It is not the night.

daydream (daydreams)

n. You have a *daydream* when you think about all sorts of lovely things that you would like to happen.

dead

adj. Something that is *dead* is not alive.

dear (dearer, dearest)

1. *adj.* If something is *dear*, it costs a lot of money to buy.
2. *adj.* If you call someone '*dear*', it shows that you like them.
3. If you say 'Oh *dear!*' you are surprised, sad or disappointed about something.

death (deaths)

n. Death is the end of life.

decay (decays, decaying, decayed)

vb. When something *decays*, it rots away.

decide (decides, deciding, decided)

vb. If you *decide* something, you make up your mind about it.

decorate (decorates, decorating, decorated)

vb. When you *decorate* something, you make it more attractive by adding something to it.

a b c **d** e f g h i j k l m

decoration (decorations)

n. A *decoration* is something colourful and pretty that you hang up when you have a celebration.

deep (deeper, deepest)

adj. If something is *deep*, it goes a long way down.

deer (deer)

n. A *deer* is a large wild animal that lives on plants. Male *deer* usually have antlers.

defend (defends, defending, defended)

vb. If you *defend* someone or something, you protect them from danger or attack.

defence (defences)

n. Your *defence* is the way you protect yourself. It could be in a time of danger or it could be in a game against another team.

delicate

1. *adj.* If something is *delicate*, it is soft and easily broken.
2. *adj.* If children are *delicate*, they easily become ill.

delicatessen (delicatessens)

n. A *delicatessen* is a shop where you can buy foods from many different countries.

delicious

adj. Something *delicious* tastes or smells very good.

delighted

adj. If you are *delighted* about something, you are very pleased about it.

deliver (delivers, delivering, delivered)

vb. If you *deliver* something to someone's house, you take it there.

delivery (deliveries)

n. A *delivery* is the bringing of letters, parcels and other things to someone's house.

demon (demons)

n. A *demon* is a bad spirit.

den (dens)

1. *n.* A *den* is a private or secret place.
2. *n.* A *den* is a wild animal's home.

dense (denser, densest)

adj. Something that is *dense*, contains a lot of things in a small area. A dense forest, for example, is very dark and thick.

dentist (dentists)

n. A *dentist* is someone whose job is to look after and treat people's teeth.

descendant (descendants)

n. A *descendant* is someone who is a member of a family that lived a long time ago.

descend (descends, descending, descended)

vb. If you *descend*, you go down.

desert (deserts)

n. A *desert* is dry, sandy or stony land where there is not much water and few plants can grow.

design (designs, designing, designed)

1. *n.* A *design* is a plan or pattern for something that shows how it can be made.
2. *vb.* If you *design* something, you make a plan or a pattern for it.

desk (desks)

n. A *desk* is a table where you can read, write or study.

a b c **d** e f g h i j k l m

despair (despairs, despairing, despaired)

1. *n. Despair* is a feeling of hopelessness.
2. *vb.* If you *despair*, you feel that nothing will ever be right again.

desperately

adv. If you want to do something *desperately*, you want to do it very badly.

destroy (destroys, destroying, destroyed)

vb. If you *destroy* something, you damage it so badly that it cannot be put right.

detach (detaches, detaching, detached)

vb. If you *detach* something, you undo or untie it so that it comes apart.

develop (develops, developing, developed)

vb. If something *develops*, it gets bigger or more important.

devil (devils)

n. A *devil* is an evil spirit.

dictionary (dictionaries)

n. A *dictionary* is a book which tells you the meaning of a word and how to spell it. A dictionary is arranged in alphabetical order.

die (dies, dying, died)

vb. When something *dies*, it stops living.

different

adj. If things are *different*, they are not the same.

difficult

adj. Something *difficult* is not easy.

dig (digs, digging, dug)

vb. When you *dig*, you move soil away to make a hole in the ground with something like a spade. When an animal *digs*, it uses its claws to make a hole.

dike (dikes)

n. A *dike* is a large ditch.

dim (dimmer, dimmest)
adj. A *dim* light is very faint.

dine (dines, dining, dined)
vb. When you *dine,* you have a meal, usually dinner.

dinner (dinners)
n. Dinner is the main meal of the day. It is sometimes eaten at midday and sometimes in the evening.

dinosaur (dinosaurs)

n. A *dinosaur* was an animal that lived on Earth in prehistoric times.

dip (dips, dipping, dipped)
vb. When you *dip* something, you quickly lower it into liquid.

direction (directions)

n. The *direction* is the way you go to get somewhere.

dirt
n. Dirt is dust or mud.

dirty (dirtier, dirtiest)
adj. A *dirty* person, animal or thing is covered with marks and is not clean.

disabled
adj. A *disabled* person has an illness or injury that stops them from moving about easily.

disappear (disappears, disappearing, disappeared)
vb. If something or someone *disappears,* they go out of sight.

disappearance (disappearances)
n. The *disappearance* of someone or something is when they cannot be found.

disaster (disasters)
n. A *disaster* is a very bad, unexpected accident (such as an earthquake).

a b c **d** e f g h i j k l m

discover (discovers, discovering, discovered)

vb. If you *discover* something you did not know before, you find out about it.

disgusting

adj. A *disgusting* thing is something that is very unpleasant.

dish (dishes)

n. A *dish* is a shallow bowl for food.

distance (distances)

n. The *distance* between two places is the amount of space between them.

distant

1. *adj.* If something is *distant*, it is very far away.
2. *adj.* A *distant* relative is a member of your family that is not very close to you.

district (districts)

n. A *district* is an area of a town or country.

ditch (ditches)

n. A *ditch* is a long, narrow channel that usually drains water away from land.

dive (dives, diving, dived)

vb. If you *dive* into water, you jump in head first.

diver (divers)

n. A *diver* is a person who explores the bottom of rivers or the sea, using special equipment for breathing.

divide (divides, dividing, divided)

1. *vb.* If you *divide* something, you make it into smaller parts.
2. *adj.* If people are *divided*, they do not agree about something.

dock (docks)

n. A *dock* is a place where ships and boats load, unload or are mended.

doctor (doctors)

n. A *doctor* is a person whose job is to help people to be well when they are ill.

dog (dogs)

n. A *dog* is a four-legged animal that people can keep as a pet. Some *dogs* guard property and some dogs can be used for hunting.

dolphin (dolphins)

n. A *dolphin* is a very intelligent mammal which lives in the sea. It looks like a fish and has a pointed mouth.

donkey (donkeys)

n. A *donkey* is an animal that looks like a small horse with long ears.

door (doors)

n. A *door* is a piece of wood, glass or metal which is used to open or close the way in to a building, a room or a cupboard.

doorbell (doorbells)

n. A *doorbell* is a bell on the outside of a building. You ring it to let people inside the building know that you are there.

double (doubles, doubling, doubled)

vb. If you *double* something, you make it twice as much.

dough

n. *Dough* is uncooked bread.

dove (doves)

n. A *dove* is a bird like a small pigeon.

down

adv. If you go *down*, you go lower.

downstairs

n. *Downstairs* is on the next floor down.

drag (drags, dragging, dragged)

vb. If you *drag* something, you pull it behind you along the ground.

a b c **d** e f g h i j k l m

dragon (dragons)

n. A *dragon* is a monster that you read about in storybooks. *Dragons* have wings and breathe fire.

drain (drains, draining, drained)

1. *n.* A *drain* is a pipe for taking away waste water.
2. *vb.* If you *drain* something, you pour liquid off slowly.

drank see **drink**

draw (draws, drawing, drew, drawn)

1. *vb.* When you *draw*, you make a picture with pencils or crayons.
2. *vb.* If a horse *draws* a cart, it pulls it along.

drawer (drawers)

n. A *drawer* is a box without a lid inside a piece of furniture.

dreadful

adj. If something is *dreadful*, it is very bad.

dream (dreams, dreaming, dreamed or dreamt)

vb. You *dream* when you hear sounds and see pictures while you are asleep.

dress (dresses, dressing, dressed)

1. *n.* A *dress* is a piece of clothing that is like a skirt and top joined together.
2. *vb.* When you *dress*, you put your clothes on.

drey (dreys)

n. A *drey* is a home for a squirrel.

dribble (dribbles, dribbling, dribbled)

vb. If you *dribble*, a little liquid trickles out of your mouth.

drift (drifts, drifting, drifted)

vb. If something or someone *drifts*, they are carried along gently by water or air.

drink (drinks, drinking, drank, drunk)

1. *n.* A *drink* is a liquid that is safe to swallow.
2. *vb.* If you *drink* something, you swallow something liquid like water.

drip (drips, dripping, dripped)

vb. If you let liquid *drip*, it falls from somewhere in small drops.

drive (drives, driving, drove, driven)
vb. If you *drive* a machine or an animal, you make it move along.

driver (drivers)

n. A *driver* is a person who drives a car, or other vehicle, on the road.

drizzle (drizzles, drizzling, drizzled)
1. *n. Drizzle* is fine rain.
2. *vb.* When it *drizzles*, fine rain falls.

drop (drops, dropping, dropped)
1. *n.* A *drop* of something is a small amount.
2. *vb.* If you *drop* something, you let it fall to the ground.

droplet (droplets)
n. A *droplet* is a tiny amount of liquid.

droppings
n. Droppings are the waste material of some small animals and birds.

drove see **drive**

drown (drowns, drowning, drowned)
vb. If you *drown*, you die because you have gone underwater and cannot breathe.

drum (drums, drumming, drummed)
1. *n.* A *drum* is a musical instrument that you bang with your hands or with sticks.
2. *vb.* If you *drum,* you beat a pattern with your hands or with sticks on something that gives out a sound.

drummer (drummers)

n. A *drummer* is a person who plays the drums.

dry (drier, driest)
adj. Something that is *dry* is not wet.

duck (ducks)
n. A *duck* is a bird that can swim and fly. It has a wide, flat beak.

duckling (ducklings)
n. A *duckling* is a baby duck.

a b c **d** e f g h i j k l m

dug see **dig**

dull (duller, dullest)
1. *adj.* A *dull* day is not sunny or very bright.
2. *adj.* A *dull* person is not very interesting.

dune (dunes)

n. A *dune* is a hill of dry sand near the sea or in the desert.

during
During means all through a particular amount of time.

dusk

n. Dusk is the time of day when the sun sets and it begins to get dark.

dust (dusts, dusting, dusted)
1. *n. Dust* is dry, powdery dirt.

2. *vb.* If you *dust* something, you clean the dust from it with a soft cloth.

duster (dusters)
n. A *duster* is a soft cloth for cleaning and polishing.

dusty (dustier, dustiest)
adj. If something is *dusty*, it has a film of dust on it.

dye (dyes, dyeing, dyed)
1. *n. Dye* is a powder that you mix with liquid. You use dye to change the colour of something.
2. *vb.* If you *dye* something, you change its colour by soaking it in dye.

E e

each

Each means every single person or thing in a group.

eagle (eagles)

n. An *eagle* is a large, strong bird that eats small animals.

ear (ears)

n. Your *ears* are on either side of your head. You use them for hearing and for balance.

early (earlier, earliest)

adv. Early is not late. If you arrive somewhere early, you get there before the time that you are expected.

earn (earns, earning, earned)

vb. If you *earn* money, you work and get paid in return.

earth

1. *n. Earth* is the ground where things grow. It is another name for soil.
2. *n.* The *Earth* is the planet that we live on.

earthquake (earthquakes)

n. An *earthquake* is a time when the ground shakes. Sometimes the shaking is so bad that buildings fall down.

earwig (earwigs)

n. An *earwig* is an insect like a small beetle with pincers at the back end of its body.

easily

adv. If you do something *easily*, you do not find it difficult to do.

east

n. *East* is one of the points of the compass.

easy (easier, easiest)

adj. If things are *easy*, they are not difficult.

eat (eats, eating, ate, eaten)

vb. If you *eat*, you take food into your body.

echo (echoes, echoing, echoed)

1. n. An *echo* is a sound that bounces back from something like the walls of a cave or a mountainside so that you can hear it again.
2. vb. If something *echoes*, you hear it again.

edge (edges)

n. The *edge* of something is the limit or end of an object or place.

edible

adj. If something is *edible*, you can eat it.

effort (efforts)

n. If you make an *effort*, you try very hard.

egg (eggs)

n. An *egg* is an oval or round object laid by birds, snakes, fish or insects. The young hatch from the *eggs* after a little time.

either

Either means one or the other of two people or things.

elastic

n. *Elastic* is a rubber material that stretches when you pull it and returns to its normal size when you let it go.

elegance

n. *Elegance* is being graceful and well-dressed.

elephant (elephants)

n. An *elephant* is the biggest animal that lives on land. It has a long nose called a trunk, and tusks.

emperor (emperors)

n. An *emperor* is a man who rules over a group of countries. An *empress* is his wife.

empty (empties, emptying, emptied; emptier, emptiest)

1. *vb.* If you *empty* something, you take everything out of it.
2. *adj.* When something is *empty*, it has nothing in it.

emu (emus)

n. An *emu* is a large bird which cannot fly. *Emus* live in Australia.

end (ends, ending, ended)

1. *n.* The *end* of something is when it finishes.
2. *n.* The *end* is the last part of something.
3. *vb.* If you *end* something, you finish it off.
4. *vb.* If a film or a television programme *ends*, it stops.

endanger (endangers, endangering, endangered)

1. *vb.* If you *endanger* something, you put it in a dangerous situation.
2. *adj.* Animals or plants which are *endangered* might be damaged so much that they will no longer exist.

enemy (enemies)

1. *n.* An *enemy* is someone who wants to harm someone else.
2. *n.* The *enemy* in a war is the opposite army.

energy (energies)

n. Energy is the strength to do things.

engine (engines)

n. An *engine* is a machine that makes its own power and is used to make things move.

engineer (engineers)

n. An *engineer* is someone who plans how roads, bridges or machines will be built.

enjoy (enjoys, enjoying, enjoyed)

vb. If you *enjoy* doing something, you are happy while you are doing it.

enormous

It's enormous!

adj. Enormous things are very, very large.

enough

n. If you have *enough* of something, you do not want or need any more.

a b c d **e** f g h i j k l m

enter (enters, entering, entered)

vb. If you *enter* a place, you go into it.

entrance (entrances)

n. The *entrance* to a place is the way in.

erupt (erupts, erupting, erupted)

vb. When a volcano *erupts*, hot lava and ashes burst out of it and pour down the sides.

escape (escapes, escaping, escaped)

vb. If you *escape*, you become free from whatever is holding you.

eskimo (eskimos)

n. An *Eskimo* is one of the people who live in the very cold parts of North America, Greenland and Russia. The *Eskimos* are also called Innuit.

especially

adv. *Especially* good means that something is very good and especially bad means that something is very bad.

even

1. *adj.* If a surface is *even*, it is flat and has no bumps in it.
2. *adj.* If you have an *even* number such as 2, 4 or 6 it can be divided by 2 and leave no remainder.

evening (evenings)

n. *Evening* is the time at the end of the day just before night.

event (events)

n. An *event* is something important that happens.

eventually

adv. *Eventually* means at last.

every

Every means all the objects or people in a group. You say *everybody* or *everyone* if you mean all the people, and *everything* if you mean all the objects. *Everywhere* means all the places.

evil (evils)

1. *n. Evil* is wickedness.
2. *adj. Evil* people do things to hurt others.

exactly

adj. If you do something *exactly,* you do it perfectly.

example (examples)

1. *n.* If you give an *example,* you show how something can be done.
2. *n.* If someone is an *example* to others, the way they behave is seen as good.

except

You say *except* when you want to leave one thing out of a list.

excite (excites, exciting, excited)

1. *vb.* If you *excite* someone, you make them very interested in what you are doing or saying.
2. *adj.* If you are *excited,* you are very happy and interested about something.

exclaim (exclaims, exclaiming, exclaimed)

vb. When you *exclaim,* you say something suddenly in a surprised way.

exclamation (exclamations)

n. An *exclamation* is a word or sound that is said suddenly and loudly, often with suprise.

exhaust (exhausts, exhausting, exhausted)

1. *n. Exhaust* is the gas or steam that comes out of a car engine.
2. *adj.* If you are *exhausted,* you are very tired.

exhaustion

n. Exhaustion is the feeling you have when you have no energy left and you are very tired.

explore (explores, exploring, explored)

vb. When you *explore,* you look around a place for the first time.

explorer (explorers)

n. An *explorer* is a person who travels to places that no one knows much about and finds out more about them.

eye (eyes)

n. The *eyes* of a person or an animal are the parts they use to see with.

extinct

adj. If an animal or plant is *extinct*, it has died out or been destroyed and no more are left.

extra

Something *extra* is more than usual.

face (faces, facing, faced)

1. *n.* Your *face* is the front part of your head where your eyes, mouth and nose are.
2. *n.* The *face* in a mine is the part of the rock from which the miners cut the coal or metal.
3. *vb.* If you *face* something difficult, you are brave about it.

fact (facts)

n. A *fact* is something that is true.

factory (factories)

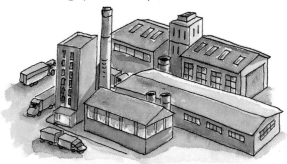

n. A *factory* is a building where goods are made by machines.

fair (fairs; fairer, fairest)

1. *n.* A *fair* is a place where there are roundabouts, stalls and rides for people to have fun. A fair travels around and stops for a few days in each place.
2. *adj.* If you are *fair*, you keep to the rules.
3. *adj.* If you have *fair* hair, it is a light colour.

fairground (fairgrounds)

n. A *fairground* is a large open space where the fair is held.

fairy (fairies)

n. A *fairy* is an imaginary creature, like a tiny human being, that you can read about in stories.

fall (falls, falling, fell, fallen)

vb. If you *fall*, you come down or drop to the ground suddenly.

false (falser, falsest)

1. *adj.* If something you say is *false*, it is not true.
2. *adj.* Something that is *false* is not the real thing.

family (families)

n. A *family* is a group of people who are related and, usually, live together and care for each other. Most *families* have a mother, a father and children.

famous

adj. If someone is *famous*, they are very well-known.

fan (fans, fanning, fanned)

1. n. If you are a *fan* of a sport or a pop group, you like them very much and are very interested in them.

2. n. A *fan* is a flat object made of folded paper that opens out. You can wave it backwards and forwards to make the air move and keep yourself cool.

3. vb. If you *fan* yourself, you keep yourself cool with a fan.

fancy (fancies, fancying, fancied)

1 vb. If you *fancy* doing something, you want to do it.

2. adj. Something that is *fancy,* is highly decorated or special in some way.

fang (fangs)

n. A *fang* is a long, sharp tooth.

fantastic

adj. If something is *fantastic*, it is wonderful and surprising.

far (farther, farthest)

adv. If a place is *far* away, it is a long way away.

farm (farms, farming, farmed)

1. n. A *farm* is a large area of land where the farmer keeps animals and grows crops like corn and vegetables. A farm has buildings on it for the farmer to live in and barns for storing crops and sheltering the animals.

2. vb. If you *farm* land, you plant crops and keep animals on it.

farmer (farmers)

n. A *farmer* is a person who looks after a farm.

farmyard (farmyards)

n. A *farmyard* is the outdoor area around the farmhouse.

fast (faster, fastest)

adj. If something is *fast*, it moves very quickly.

fasten (fastens, fastening, fastened)

vb. When you *fasten* something, you close it or do it up with something like a button, a zip or a catch.

fat (fatter, fattest)

adj. If a person or animal is *fat*, they are very big and have a lot of flesh on their body.

father (fathers)

n. A *father* is a man who has his own child or children.

fault (faults)

n. A *fault* is a mistake.

faun (fauns)

n. A *faun* is an imaginary creature that looks like a man with goat's legs and horns.

favourite

adj. Your *favourite* thing is the one you like the best.

fawn (fawns)

n. A *fawn* is a young deer.

fear (fears, fearing, feared)

1. *n.* *Fear* is an unpleasant feeling you have when you are in danger or in pain.
2. *vb.* If you *fear* someone or something, you are afraid of them.

fearsome

adj. Something *fearsome* is very scary and frightening.

feast (feasts, feasting, feasted)

1. *n.* A *feast* is a large meal for lots of people.
2. *vb.* If you *feast*, you eat a great deal of food.

feather (feathers)

n. A *feather* is one of the many very light pieces that make up the covering of a bird's body.

feathery

adj. If something is *feathery*, it is very soft and light.

feed (feeds, feeding, fed)

vb. When you *feed* someone, you give them something to eat.

feel (feels, feeling, felt)

vb. If you *feel* sad, happy or ill, that is the way you are at the time.

a b c d e **f** g h i j k l m

feeler (feelers)

n. An insect's *feelers* are the two long, thin stalks that stick out on the top of its head. The insect uses them to touch and sense things around it.

feeling (feelings)

n. Your *feelings* are the way you feel in your mind. You can be happy, sad, calm or angry.

feet see **foot**

fell see **fall**

fellow (fellows)

n. A *fellow* is another name for a man.

felt see **feel**

female (females)

n. Any person or animal that is *female* can have babies.

fence (fences)

n. A *fence* is something that divides two pieces of land. It can be made of wire or of wood.

feral

adj. Feral animals are animals which used to be kept by people but have become wild.

ferry (ferries)

n. A *ferry* is a boat that takes people and cars across a stretch of water.

ferryman (ferrymen)

n. A *ferryman* operates a ferry.

festival (festivals)

n. A *festival* is a time or an event when people do special things together to celebrate something.

fetch (fetches, fetching, fetched)

vb. When you *fetch* something, you go and get it.

fête (fêtes)

n. A *fête* is a kind of open-air party with competitions and stalls selling cakes, toys and many other things.

fever (fevers)

n. When you have a *fever*, you are ill with a high temperature.

few (fewer, fewest)

adj. A *few* things are not very many.

fibre (fibres)

n. A *fibre* is a thin thread of something like wool, cotton or nylon.

fiddle (fiddles)

n. A *fiddle* is another name for a violin.

fiddler (fiddlers)

n. Someone who plays a fiddle is called a *fiddler*.

field (fields)

n. A *field* is a piece of land with a fence or a hedge around it.

fierce (fiercer, fiercest)

adj. An animal or person that is *fierce*, looks and sounds angry.

fig (figs)

n. A *fig* is a soft, sweet fruit that grows in hot countries. It is shaped like a small pear.

fight (fights, fighting, fought)

1. *vb.* When people or animals *fight*, they try to hurt each other.
2. If you *fight* an illness, you try to get better.

fill (fills, filling, filled)

vb. If you *fill* something, you put so much in that there is no room for more. It is full.

film (films)

n. A *film* is a moving picture which tells a story and which is shown on a screen. Well-known people or animals who appear in *films* are called film stars.

finally

adv. If someone *finally* does something, they do it after a long time of trying to do it.

find (finds, finding, found)

vb. If you *find* something, you see it or come across it after you have been looking for it.

a b c d e **f** g h i j k l m

fine (finer, finest)

1. *adj. Fine* things are of very good quality indeed.
2. *adj.* If the weather is *fine*, it is sunny and dry.
3. *adj.* If sugar or sand is *fine*, all the grains in it are very small in size.
4. *adj.* If you feel *fine*, you feel all right.

finger (fingers)

n. Your *finger* is one of the long, thin parts at the end of your hand that you use to feel and hold things.

finish (finishes, finishing, finished)

vb. If you *finish* something, you have come to the end.

fire (fires)

1. *n.* A *fire* is a burning pile of wood or coal to keep people warm or to cook food over.
2. *n.* A *fire* is something powered by gas or electricity to keep people warm.
3. *n. Fire* is the bright light and heat from something burning.

fire fighter (fire fighters)

n. A *fire fighter* is a person who puts out fires or helps people who are trapped. *Fire fighters* are based at a fire station and use a fire engine to get to fires quickly.

firm (firmer, firmest)

vb. If something is *firm*, it does not give way when you press it, but it is not quite hard.

first

adv. If you are *first*, you are before everyone else.

fish (fish or fishes; fishing, fished)

1. *n.* A *fish* is a creature with scales and fins that lives under water and breathes through gills.
2. *vb.* If you *fish*, you try to catch fish in a river, pond or at sea.

fisherman (fishermen)

n. A *fisherman* catches fish for a living or for sport.

fishmonger (fishmongers)

n. A *fishmonger* sells fish for people to eat.

flag (flags)

n. A *flag* is a piece of cloth with a special design on it to show who it belongs to.

flame (flames)

n. A *flame* is a tongue of fire. Something that is in *flames* is on fire.

flan (flans)

n. A *flan* is a pie with no lid. It can be filled with fruit or with savoury things.

flannel (flannels)

n. A *flannel* is a piece of cloth that you use when you wash.

flap (flaps, flapping, flapped)

vb. If a bird *flaps* its wings, it makes them move up and down.

flapjack (flapjacks)

n. A *flapjack* is a thick chewy biscuit made from oats, butter and syrup or treacle.

flash (flashes, flashing, flashed)

1. *n.* A *flash* is a sudden bright light that last for just a moment, like a flash of lightning.
2. If something happens in a *flash*, it happens very quickly.

flat (flats; flatter, flattest)

1. *n.* A *flat* is a group of rooms on one floor in a large building for people to live in.
2. *adj.* If something is *flat*, it has no bumps in it.

flesh

n. The *flesh* of a person or an animal is the soft part that covers the bones.

flew see **fly**

flick (flicks, flicking, flicked)

vb. If you *flick* something, you make it move quickly and suddenly by using your fingers.

flicker (flickers, flickering, flickered)

vb. If a light *flickers*, it goes on and off, changing in brightness.

a b c d e **f** g h i j k l m

flies see **fly**

flipper (flippers)

   1. *n*. The *flippers* of an animal are the flat feet that they use for swimming.

   2. *n*. *Flippers* are flat pieces of rubber that you can wear on your feet to help you to swim more quickly.

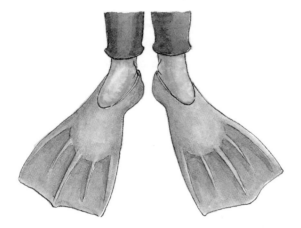

float (floats, floating, floated)

   vb. If something *floats*, it rests on the top of a liquid.

flock (flocks, flocking, flocked)

   1. *n*. A *flock* is a group of sheep or birds gathered together.

   2. *vb*. If people, animals or birds *flock*, they gather together in one place.

flood (floods, flooding, flooded)

   1. *n*. A *flood* is a huge amount of water that spreads over a large area of land which is usually dry.

   2. *vb*. If a river *floods*, the water spreads all over the land around it.

floor (floors)

   n. The *floor* is the flat part of a room that people walk on.

flour

   n. *Flour* is a white or brown powder made from grinding grain such as wheat. Flour is used to make things like bread and cakes.

flower (flowers, flowering, flowered)

   1. *n*. A *flower* is the part of a plant or tree that holds seeds. It is usually brightly coloured and lasts for a short time.

   2. *vb*. When a plant or tree *flowers*, the buds open.

fluff

   n. *Fluff* is light soft stuff that comes off wool, cotton, fur and hair. If something is fluffy, it is soft and woolly.

fluke (flukes)

   1. *n*. *Flukes* are the two points of a whale's tail.

   2. *n*. A *fluke* is a bit of luck that helps you to do something that you thought you could not do.

flute (flutes)

n. A *flute* is a musical instrument shaped like a pipe with holes in it. You play it by blowing into it. You change the notes by putting your fingers over the different holes.

flutter (flutters, fluttering, fluttered)

1. *vb.* If a bird or insect *flutters*, it makes small, quick movements with its wings.
2. *vb.* If something *flutters* in the wind, it moves very gently.

fly (flies, flying, flew, flown)

1. *n.* A *fly* is a small insect with one pair of wings.
2. *n.* If a bird or a plane *flies*, it travels through the air.

fodder

n. *Fodder* is food for cattle or horses.

fog (fogs)

n. *Fog* is a very thick mist made up of many tiny droplets of water.

foil (foils, foiling, foiled)

1. *n.* *Foil* is thin, metal paper which is used to wrap food.
2. *vb.* If you *foil* someone's plan, you find out about it and stop them from doing it.

fold (folds, folding, folded)

1. *n.* A *fold* is a curve where paper or material has been bent over itself.
2. *vb.* If you *fold* something, you bend it so that one part covers the other.

folk (folks)

n. *Folk* is an old-fashioned word for people.

follow (follows, following, followed)

1. *vb.* If you *follow* someone or something, you go after them.
2. *vb.* If you *follow* a path, you go along it.

fond (fonder, fondest)

adj. If you are *fond* of someone or something, you like them very much.

food (foods)

n. *Food* is what we eat to help us to grow.

foot (feet)

n. Your *foot* is part of your body. It joins your leg at your ankle.

a b c d e **f** g h i j k l m

football (footballs)

1. *n. Football* is a game that is played by two teams who try to score goals by kicking a ball into a net.
2. *n.* A *football* is the name of the ball that is used for playing the game of football.

footprint (footprints)

n. A *footprint* is a mark in the shape of a foot that a person or animal makes on something.

forecast (forecasts, forecasting, forecasted)

1. *n.* A *forecast* tells you what is expected to happen. A weather forecast tells us what the weather is expected to be like.
2. *vb.* If you *forecast* something, you say what you think is going to happen in the future.

forest (forests)

n. A *forest* is a large area where trees grow closely together.

forever

adv. Something which goes on *forever*, never seems to end.

forget (forgets, forgetting, forgot, forgotten)

vb. When you *forget* something, you do not remember it even though you knew it before.

forgive (forgives, forgiving, forgiven, forgave)

vb. If you *forgive* someone for something wrong that they have done, you are not cross with them anymore.

fork (forks)

n. A *fork* is a tool with points at the end of it that you use for eating.

form (forms, forming, formed)

1. *n.* A *form* is a piece of paper that you fill in to give information about yourself.
2. *vb.* If you *form* something, you make it into a particular shape.

fortune (fortunes)

1. *n.* Your *fortune* is the good or bad luck you have in life.
2. *n.* If you have a *fortune*, you have a very large amount of money.

forward (forwards)

adv. If you move *forward*, you go in the direction you are facing.

fossil (fossils)

n. A *fossil* is the hardened remains of a prehistoric plant or animal that is found inside rock.

fought see **fight**

found see **find**

foundation (foundations)

n. The *foundations* of a building are the solid parts underground that stop it falling down.

fountain (fountains)

n. A *fountain* is a jet or spray of water which spouts up in the middle of a pool or a lake.

fox (foxes)

n. A *fox* is a wild animal which looks like a dog. It has reddish-brown fur and a bushy tail.

fragile

adj. Something that is *fragile* is easily damaged or broken.

fray (frays, fraying, frayed)

vb. If something *frays*, it wears ragged at the edges.

freak (freaks)

n. If something is a *freak*, it is unexpected or unusual.

free (frees, freeing, freed)

1. *vb.* If you *free* someone or something, you let it go.
2. *adj.* If you are *free*, there is nothing to stop you from doing anything you want to do.
3. *adj.* If something is *free*, you do not have to pay for it.

a b c d e **f** g h i j k l m

freeze (freezes, freezing, froze, frozen)

vb. If liquid *freezes*, it becomes solid because the temperature is so low.

fresh (fresher, freshest)

adj. If something is *fresh*, it is new.

fridge (fridges)

n. A *fridge* is a large, metal container. It is kept cool so that the food in it stays fresh.

friend (friends)

n. A *friend* is someone you like and who likes you too.

friendly (friendlier, friendliest)

adj. Someone who is *friendly* behaves in a kind, pleasant way to other people.

fright (frights)

1. *n.* *Fright* is a sudden feeling of fear.
2. *n.* If you have a *fright*, something makes you jump.

frighten (frightens, frightening, frightened)

1. *vb.* If you *frighten* someone, you make them feel afraid.
2. *adj.* Something *frightening* upsets and worries you.

frog (frogs)

n. A *frog* is a small animal with smooth skin, big eyes and long back legs which it uses for jumping. *Frogs* live near water.

front (fronts)

n. The *front* of something is the part that you usually see first. It is the part that faces you.

frozen see **freeze**

fruit (fruit or fruits)

n. *Fruit* is the part of a tree or plant that holds the seeds. You can often eat the juicy part around the seeds or the stone.

fry (fries, frying, fried)

vb. If you *fry* something, you cook it in a pan with hot fat.

full (fuller, fullest)

adj. If something is *full*, there is no room for anything else to fit in.

fun

n. Having *fun* is enjoying yourself and doing things that make you happy.

funny (funnier, funniest)

adj. *Funny* things are amusing and make you laugh.

fur (furs)

n. *Fur* is the soft, hairy covering on an animal's skin.

furious

adj. If you are *furious*, you are really angry.

furniture

n. *Furniture* means things like beds, tables, chairs and cupboards that you need in a house and that you can move about.

furry (furrier, furriest)

adj. *Furry* things are covered in fur.

fuss (fusses, fussing, fussed)

vb. If you *fuss*, you worry too much about something that is not important.

G g

gadget (gadgets)

n. A *gadget* is a small and useful piece of machinery.

gallop (gallops, galloping, galloped)

vb. If a horse *gallops*, it moves very quickly.

game (games)

1. *n.* A *game* is something you play for fun. It can be with toys or you can pretend to be someone else.
2. *n.* A *game* is a sport that you play with rules. You use your skill to try to win.

garden (gardens, gardening, gardened)

1. *n.* A *garden* is land next to someone's house where they can grow flowers, trees and vegetables.
2. *vb.* If you *garden*, you look after all the things growing in the garden.

gardener (gardeners)

n. A *gardener* is a person who looks after other people's gardens as a job.

gas (gases)

n. Gas is like air. It can burn easily and is used as fuel for fires, cookers and central heating.

gasp (gasps, gasping, gasped)

1. *n.* A *gasp* is a short, quick breath of air.
2. *vb.* If you *gasp*, you take a short, quick breath.

gate (gates)

n. A *gate* is like a door in a fence or a wall.

gather (gathers, gathering, gathered)

vb. If people or animals *gather*, they come together in a group.

gave see **give**

geese see **goose**

general (generals)
   n. A *general* is an important person in the army.

generator (generators)
   n. A *generator* is a machine that makes electricity.

gentle (gentler, gentlest)
   1. *adj.* A *gentle* touch is soft, quiet and light.
   2. *adj.* A *gentle* person is quiet and kind.

gentleman (gentlemen)
   n. A *gentleman* is a polite name for a man.

gently
   adv. If you speak *gently*, you speak softly and quietly. If you touch someone or something *gently*, you touch them carefully.

ghost (ghosts)
   n. A *ghost* is a dead person that some people think they can see or feel near to them.

giant (giants)
   n. In fairy stories, a *giant* is a huge person.

gift (gifts)
   n. A *gift* is a present.

giggle (giggles, giggling, giggled)
   vb. When you *giggle*, you laugh in a silly way.

ginger
   n. *Ginger* is a spice used to make some foods hot.

gingerbread
   n. *Gingerbread* is a sweet cake or biscuit made with ginger.

giraffe (giraffes)
   n. A *giraffe* is a large African animal. It has a very long neck, long legs and dark patches on yellowish skin.

girl (girls)

n. A *girl* is a female child.

give (gives, giving, gave, given)

vb. If you *give* someone something, you let them have it.

glad (gladder, gladdest)

adj. When you are *glad*, you are happy about something.

gland (glands)

n. A *gland* is an organ in the body that makes substances for the body to use.

glass (glasses)

1. *n. Glass* is something hard that you can see through. It is easily broken. Clear glass is used to make windows and dishes. Coloured glass is sometimes used to make ornaments and marbles.
2. *n. Glasses* are what people with poor eyesight wear, to help them to see better.

gleam (gleams, gleaming, gleamed)

vb. When something *gleams*, it shines.

glide (glides, gliding, glided)

vb. When you *glide*, you move very smoothly.

glockenspiel (glockenspiels)

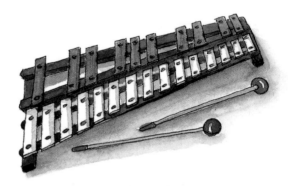

n. A *glockenspiel* is a musical instrument with bells or bars that you play by striking them with special hammers.

gloomy (gloomier, gloomiest)

1. *adj.* When the weather is cloudy and *gloomy*, it is dark.
2. *adj.* If you feel *gloomy*, you feel sad.

glossary (glossaries)

n. A *glossary* is an alphabetical list of words with their meanings that you find at the back of a book.

glossy (glossier, glossiest)

adj. If something is *glossy*, it is shiny and smooth.

glove (gloves)

n. A *glove* is a covering for your hand to protect it or to keep it warm.

glow (glows, glowing, glowed)

vb. If something *glows*, it shines with a warm light.

gnome (gnomes)

n. A *gnome* is a small, imaginary old man with a beard. You can read about *gnomes* in some stories.

goat (goats)

n. A *goat* is an animal that is kept mainly for its milk. It has coarse hair, horns and a short tail.

gobble (gobbles, gobbling, gobbled)

vb. If you *gobble* your food, you eat it very quickly.

God

n. Christians, Jews and Muslims believe that *God* made the world and rules over it.

god (gods)

n. A *god* is a spirit in some religions who is worshipped as being powerful.

godmother (godmothers)

n. A *godmother* is a woman who promises at a christening in a Christian church to see that the child is brought up as a Christian.

gold

n. *Gold* is a valuable, yellow metal used for making coins and jewels.

golden

adj. Something that is *golden* is the colour of gold.

good (better, best)

1. *adj.* If a child or animal is *good*, they are well-behaved.
2. *adj.* If music, painting or a play is *good*, it is enjoyable and well-done.
3. *adj.* Someone who is caring and kind is *good*.

goods

n. *Goods* are things that can be bought and sold.

a b c d e f **g** h i j k l m

goodbye (goodbyes)

'Goodbye' is what you say when you leave someone.

goodnight (goodnights)

'Goodnight' is what you say when you leave someone at night.

goose (geese)

n. A *goose* is a large bird that swims, flies and lays eggs. *Geese* are bigger than ducks and have long beaks. They are very bad-tempered and are sometimes used to guard houses in the country.

gorilla (gorillas)

n. A *gorilla* is the largest of the apes. *Gorillas* live in African forests in family groups. They eat fruit and leaves.

grab (grabs, grabbing, grabbed)

vb. If you *grab* something, you take hold of it suddenly.

graceful

adj. If you are *graceful*, you move in an elegant and smooth way.

gradually

adv. If you do something *gradually*, you do it bit by bit.

grand (grander, grandest)

adj. If something is *grand*, it is important and splendid.

grandfather (grandfathers)

n. Your *grandfather* is the father of your mother or your father. Some people call their grandfather grandpa or grandad.

grandmother (grandmothers)

n. Your *grandmother* is the mother of your mother or your father. Some people call their grandmother grandma, nanny or granny.

grape (grapes)

n. A *grape* is a small, soft, green or purple fruit that grows in bunches.

graph (graphs)

n. A *graph* is a chart that gives information.

grass (grasses)

n. Grass is the plant with thin, green leaves that grows thickly in fields and on lawns and hillsides. Cattle and other animals eat grass.

grasshopper (grasshoppers)

n. A *grasshopper* is an insect with very long back legs which can jump into the air.

grate (grates, grating, grated)

vb. If you *grate* vegetables or cheese, you shred them into small pieces.

graze (grazes, grazing, grazed)

1. *vb.* If you *graze* yourself, you scrape your skin in a fall.
2. *vb.* If a cow or other animal *grazes*, it spends a long time eating grass.

great (greater, greatest)

adj. Great is something very big, grand and wonderful.

grease

n. Grease is a thick oil which is used to keep the moving parts of a machine working.

greedy (greedier, greediest)

adj. Greedy people and animals eat more than they need.

green (greener, greenest)

adj. Something that is *green* is the colour of grass and trees.

greet (greets, greeting, greeted)

vb. When you *greet* someone, you say hello to them.

grew see grow

grey (greyer, greyest)

adj. Something that is *grey* is the colour of the sky when it rains.

grill (grills, grilling, grilled)

vb. When you *grill* food, you cook it with the heat coming from above.

grin (grins, grinning, grinned)

vb. If you *grin*, you give a wide smile.

groan (groans, groaning, groaned)
vb. If you *groan*, you make a low moaning sound because you are unhappy or in pain.

ground
n. Ground is the earth under your feet.

group (groups)
n. A *group* is a number of people or things which are together in one place.

grow (grows, growing, grew, grown)
vb. If something *grows*, it gets bigger.

growl (growls, growling, growled)
vb. If a dog *growls*, it makes a deep, rumbling, angry sound.

grub (grubs)
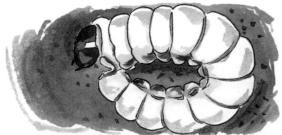
n. A *grub* is a young insect which has just come out of the egg. A grub looks like a small, fat worm.

grumble (grumbles, grumbling, grumbled)
vb. When you *grumble*, you complain and moan about something.

grumpy (grumpier, grumpiest)
adj. When you are *grumpy*, you are bad-tempered and cross.

grunt (grunts, grunting, grunted)
1. *n.* A *grunt* is a low, snorting noise.
2. *vb.* When an animal *grunts*, it makes a noise like a pig.

guard (guards, guarding, guarded)

1. *n.* A *guard* is a person who watches over people, places or objects to keep them safe.
2. *vb.* If you *guard* something, you look after it and protect it.

guess (guesses, guessing, guessed)
1. *n.* If you make a *guess*, you give an answer to a question when you do not really know the answer.
2. *vb.* If you *guess*, you try to give an answer although you do not have all the information you need.

guide (guides, guiding, guided)
1. *n.* A *guide* is a person who shows people the way to go.
2. *vb.* If you *guide* someone, you show them the way or how to do something.

guitar (guitars)

n. A *guitar* is a musical instrument with strings. You play it with your fingers.

gulp (gulps, gulping, gulped)
vb. If you *gulp,* you swallow quickly or swallow a large amount of food or drink at once.

gum (gums)
1. *n.* Your *gums* are the firm pink flesh around your teeth.

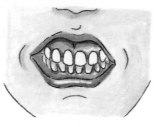

2. *n.* *Gum* is a sticky sweet that you have to chew a lot.

gun (guns)
n. A *gun* is a weapon that shoots bullets.

gurgle (gurgles, gurgling, gurgled)
vb. If water *gurgles,* it makes a noise like the bath water running out.

guy (guys)
n. You can call a group of friends '*guys*'. They can be boys or girls.

H h

habitat (habitats)

n. The *habitat* is the natural home of a plant or animal.

hail (hails, hailing, hailed)

1. *n.* *Hail* is frozen rain.
2. *vb.* When it *hails*, small frozen balls of water fall from the sky as hailstones.

hair (hair or hairs)

n. *Hair* grows on the heads and bodies of people and animals. It is made up of many fine threads.

hairy (hairier, hairiest)

adj. Someone or something that has a great deal of hair is *hairy*.

half (halves)

n. If you cut something exactly through the middle, you cut it in *half*. Two *halves* are equal.

hall (halls)

n. The *hall* in a house is the part inside the front door that leads to other rooms.

hammer (hammers, hammering, hammered)

1. *n.* A *hammer* is a tool with a handle and a heavy head for hitting nails.
2. *vb.* When you *hammer* something, you hit it with a hammer.

hand (hands)

n. Your *hand* is at the end of your arm. It has four fingers and a thumb.

handle (handles, handling, handled)

1. *n.* A *handle* on a door or window is the knob or lever that you move to open or close it.
2. *vb.* If you *handle* something, you touch, feel or hold it with your hands.

handsome

adj. Someone who is *handsome* is good-looking.

hang (hangs, hanging, hanged, hung)

vb. If you *hang* something up, you put it on a hook so it does not touch the ground.

happen (happens, happening, happened)

vb. If something *happens*, it takes place.

happy (happier, happiest)

adj. If you are *happy*, you are enjoying yourself and feel pleased about life.

harbour (harbours)

n. A *harbour* is a place where ships and boats can unload and where they can shelter from storms.

hard (harder, hardest)

1. *adj.* If something is *hard*, it is not soft.
2. *adj.* If something is *hard* to do, it is difficult.

hare (hares)

n. A *hare* is an animal like a large rabbit, with long ears and long legs. It can move very fast.

harm (harms, harming, harmed)

vb. If you *harm* someone or something, you hurt them.

harness (harnesses)

n. A *harness* is a set of straps that is put over a horse's head and neck.

a b c d e f g **h** i j k l m

harp (harps)

n. A *harp* is a large musical instrument with strings.

hat (hats)

n. A *hat* is a covering for your head when you go outside.

hatch (hatches, hatching, hatched)

vb. When something *hatches*, it comes out of an egg.

hate (hates, hating, hated)

vb. If you *hate* someone, you do not like them at all.

hawk (hawks)

n. A *hawk* is a large bird which catches small animals for food. A hawk is a bird of prey.

hay

n. *Hay* is dry grass which is fed to animals. Large amounts of hay are gathered together and made into a haystack.

haze

n. A *haze* is damp or hot air which makes a mist.

head (heads)

n. Your *head* is the part of your body that holds your brain, eyes, nose, mouth and ears.

headache (headaches)

n. A *headache* is a pain in your head.

health

n. *Health* is how your body feels. When you are well, you are healthy.

heap (heaps, heaping, heaped)

1. *n.* A *heap* of something is a pile of it.
2. *vb.* If you *heap* things up, you pile them on top of each other.

hear (hears, hearing, heard)

vb. When you *hear* things, you notice sounds through your ears.

heart (hearts)

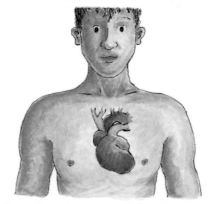

n. Your *heart* pumps blood around your body.

heat (heats, heating, heated)
1. *n. Heat* is warmth.
2. *vb.* If you *heat* something, you make it hot.

heaven (heavens)
n. Heaven is a place where happiness never ends. Many people believe that God lives there and that people who are good go to heaven when they die.

heavy (heavier, heaviest)
adj. Something *heavy* is difficult to lift or carry.

hedge (hedges)
n. A *hedge* is a kind of wall made of bushes or small trees growing close to each other.

hedgehog (hedgehogs)

n. A *hedgehog* is a small brown animal which is covered in prickles.

heir (heirs)
n. An *heir* is a boy or man who inherits money, goods or other things when someone dies. A girl or woman is called an *heiress*.

helicopter (helicopters)

n. A *helicopter* is an aircraft that flies using a large set of blades on its roof. It can take off and land in a very small space.

hello (hellos)
'*Hello*' is a way of greeting people.

helmet (helmets)
n. A *helmet* is a special hat that protects the head.

help (helps, helping, helped)
1. *vb.* If you *help* someone, you make things easier for them.
2. If you call out '*Help!*', you want to be heard because you are in danger and you want someone to rescue you.

hen (hens)
n. A *hen* is a chicken that lays eggs.

herb (herbs)
n. A *herb* is a plant that can be used for cooking or for making medicine.

herd (herds, herding, herded)

1. *n.* A *herd* is a group of animals that are kept together. A herdsman looks after the herd as his job.
2. *vb.* If you *herd* people or animals, you gather them together as a group.

hermit (hermits)

n. A *hermit* is a person who lives alone in a place far away from anyone else.

hero (heroes)

n. A *hero* is a boy or a man who has done something very brave. A girl or woman who does something very brave is called a *heroine*.

herring (herring or herrings)

n. A *herring* is a long silver-coloured sea fish that you can eat.

hibernate (hibernates, hibernating, hibernated)

vb. When animals *hibernate*, they spend the winter in a deep sleep and do not need any food.

hiccup (hiccups, hiccuping, hiccuped)

1. *n.* A *hiccup* is a short, sharp sound that comes from your throat.
2. *vb.* If you *hiccup*, you make several short, sharp, sounds from your throat.

hide (hides, hiding, hid, hidden)

vb. If you *hide* from someone, you get into a place where no one can see you.

high (higher, highest)

adj. Something that is *high* goes up a long way.

hill (hills)

n. A *hill* is ground which is higher than the ground around it.

hippopotamus (hippopotamuses or hippopotami)

n. A *hippopotamus* is a large, heavy African animal that spends a great deal of time in rivers and lakes.

hiss (hisses, hissing, hissed)

  1. *n.* A *hiss* is a long sound like a 'S'.

  2. *vb.* If you *hiss*, you make a sound like a snake.

history (histories)

  n. *History* is what happened in the past.

hit (hits, hitting, hit)

  vb. If you *hit* something or someone, you strike them or knock them.

hive (hives)

  n. A *hive* is a place for bees to live. It looks like a box. On the inside there are places for the bees to build their honeycombs.

hold (holds, holding, held)

  vb. If you *hold* something, you take it and keep it in your hand.

hole (holes)

  n. A *hole* is an opening in something.

holiday (holidays)

  n. A *holiday* is time off from school or work when people rest and enjoy themselves.

hollow (hollows; hollower, hollowest)

  1. *adj.* If something is *hollow*, it has an empty space inside it.

  2. *adj.* If a sound is *hollow*, it goes on for a long time like an echo.

holly (hollies)

  n. *Holly* is a small, evergreen tree that has red berries and prickly, shiny leaves.

home (homes)

  n. A *home* is a place to live.

honey

  n. *Honey* is the sweet yellow liquid that bees make. People often eat honey on bread.

hop (hops, hopping, hopped)

  vb. If you *hop*, you jump about on one foot.

hope (hopes, hoping, hoped)
vb. If you *hope* for something, you wish it will happen.

horn (horns)

1. *n.* A *horn* is a hard pointed growth on the top of the heads of certain animals.
2. *n.* A *horn* is what you can press in a vehicle to make a warning sound.

horrible
adj. Horrible things or people are nasty or frightening.

horror (horrors)
n. Horror is a strong feeling that you get when something is very frightening or shocking.

horse (horses)
n. A *horse* is a large animal which people ride. Some *horses* are used for pulling coaches, carts or ploughs.

hospital (hospitals)
n. A *hospital* is a place where people go to be cared for when they are sick or hurt.

hot (hotter, hottest)
adj. Something *hot* is very warm.

hotel (hotels)
n. A *hotel* is a large house where people can pay for their rooms and meals and stay for one or more nights.

hour (hours)
n. An *hour* is a length of time. An hour is 60 minutes. A day has 24 *hours.*

house (houses)
n. A *house* is a building where people live together.

household (households)
n. A *household* is everyone who lives in one house.

howl (howls, howling, howled)
vb. If an animal *howls,* it makes long crying sounds over and over again.

huddle (huddles, huddling, huddled)
vb. If people *huddle,* they get together in a tight group.

hug (hugs, hugging, hugged)
vb. When you *hug* someone, you put your arms around them and give them a squeeze.

huge (huger, hugest)

adj. Something *huge* is very, very big.

hull (hulls)

n. A *hull* is the frame of a ship.

human (humans)

n. A *human* is a man, woman or child.

hump (humps)

n. A *hump* is a big lump. A camel has a hump on its back.

hung see **hang**

hungry (hungrier, hungriest)

adj. If you are *hungry*, your stomach feels empty and you want something to eat.

hunt (hunts, hunting, hunted)

1. *n.* When a group of people search for the same thing, they have a *hunt*. A treasure hunt is a party game when everyone looks for the prize.
2. *vb.* When you *hunt* for something, you look carefully for it.

3. *vb.* People who *hunt* wild animals go after them to trap or kill them.

hunter (hunters)

n. A *hunter* is a person who goes hunting. People who hunt on horseback are called huntsmen.

hurricane (hurricanes)

n. A *hurricane* is a violent storm with a strong wind that does a great deal of damage.

hurry (hurries, hurrying, hurried)

vb. If you *hurry*, you move very quickly so you will not be late.

hurt (hurts, hurting, hurt)

vb. If you *hurt* yourself, you feel pain.

hut (huts)

n. A *hut* is a small house with only one or two rooms.

hutch (hutches)

n. A *hutch* is a home for a rabbit.

hyena (hyenas)

n. A *hyena* is an animal that looks like a dog. *Hyenas* hunt in packs. They live in Africa.

a b c d e f g **h** **i** j k l m

ice

n. Ice is water that has frozen hard.

ice-cream (ice-creams)

n. Ice-cream is a sweet, frozen food that tastes creamy. There are many different flavours of ice-cream such as strawberry, chocolate and toffee.

icing

n. Icing is a sweet, sugary covering for a cake.

idea (ideas)

n. An *idea* is something that you, or someone else, thinks of.

ignore (ignores, ignoring, ignored)

vb. If you *ignore* someone, you take no notice of them.

ill

adj. If you are *ill*, there is something wrong with you. You may have an illness like measles or flu.

imagine (imagines, imagining, imagined)

vb. When you *imagine* something, you think about it so that you have a clear picture of it in your head.

immediately

adv. If you do something *immediately*, you do it straight away.

important

adj. Something or someone *important* is special, clever or powerful.

impossible

adj. Something that is *impossible*, cannot be done.

impressive

adj. If something is *impressive*, many people admire it and will never forget it.

inch (inches)

n. An *inch* is a measurement of length equal to 2.54 centimetres.

include (includes, including, included)

vb. When you *include* people or things in something, you make sure that they are all part of it.

incredible

adj. If something is *incredible*, it is difficult to believe.

indeed

You say '*indeed*' to show that you agree with something that has been said.

index (indexes)

n. An *index* is a list at the back of a book. It is in alphabetical order and tells you where to find things in the book.

individual (individuals)

n. An *individual* is a person who is separate and different from every other person.

information

n. Information is a collection of words that tell you about something or someone.

ingredient (ingredients)

n. Ingredients are all the things that have to be mixed together to make something.

initial (initials)

n. Initials are the first letters of words. For example, G and L are the initials of this dictionary writer!

inland

n. Inland means away from the sea.

a b c d e f g h i j k l m

inn (inns)

n. An *inn* is an old hotel where people can pay to stay the night and have a meal or a drink in the bar.

insect (insects)

n. An *insect* is a small creature with six legs and its skeleton on the outside. Ants, flies and beetles are *insects*.

insecticide (insecticides)

n. An *insecticide* is something which is used to kill insects when they are in places where they do damage.

inside (insides)

adv. If someone or something is *inside*, they are indoors or in it.

instrument (instruments)

1. n. An *instrument* is an object that you use for doing something.

2. n. An *instrument* is an object that you use to make music.

insulate (insulates, insulating, insulated)

vb. If you *insulate* something, you wrap it up so that it will not get cold or so that electricity will not escape.

interest (interests, interesting, interested)

1. n. If you have an *interest* in something, you want to learn or hear more about it.
2. adj. Things that are *interesting* make you want to find out more about them.

introduction (introductions)

n. The *introduction* to something is at the beginning. If a book has an introduction it tells you about what is in it.

invade (invades, invading, invaded)

vb. When one country or group of people *invades* another, they move into it to try to take it over.

invention (inventions)

n. An *invention* is something that no-one else has thought of before.

invitation (invitations)

n. An *invitation* asks you to come to something, like a party or a wedding.

invite (invites, inviting, invited)

vb. If you *invite* someone to do something, you ask them if they would like to do it.

iron (irons, ironing, ironed)

1. *n.* An *iron* is an object that you heat up and use to smooth the creases out of your clothes.
2. *n.* *Iron* is a strong, hard metal.
3. *vb.* When you *iron* something, you use an iron to smooth the creases out of your clothes.

irrigate (irrigates, irrigating, irrigated)

vb. If you *irrigate* dry land, you bring water to it along ditches so that plants can grow.

island (islands)

n. An *island* is a piece of land with water all around it.

isle (isles)

n. An *isle* is a small island.

ivory (ivories)

n. *Ivory* is a creamy-white type of bone. Elephants' tusks are made of ivory.

jack (jacks)

n. A *jack* is an object that you use to lift up a car while you change a tyre.

jacket (jackets)

n. A *jacket* is a piece of clothing which is like a short coat.

jam (jams)

n. Jam is made from fruit boiled with sugar until it is thick. Jam is spread on bread or cakes.

jar (jars)

n. A *jar* is a glass container.

jaw (jaws)

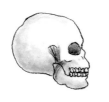 

n. Your *jaw* is one of the bones in your mouth that hold your teeth.

jealous

adj. If you feel *jealous,* you feel unhappy because someone else has something that you think you should have.

jeans

n. Jeans are trousers made from thick, hard-wearing cloth.

jelly (jellies)

n. Jelly is a soft, sweet food which wobbles when you move it.

jellyfish

n. A *jellyfish* is a sea-creature which has a body that looks like clear jelly.

Jesus

n. Jesus is the name of the man who Christians believe is the son of God.

jet (jets)

n. A *jet* is a very fast plane.

jetty (jetties)

n. A *jetty* is a small landing platform by the sea or on a river.

jewel (jewels)

n. A *jewel* is a precious stone.

jiggle (jiggles, jiggling, jiggled)
vb. If you *jiggle*, you wriggle and hop about.

job (jobs)
1. *n.* A *job* is work that someone does for money.
2. *n.* A *job* is something that has to be done.

jog (jogs, jogging, jogged)
vb. When you *jog*, you run gently and slowly to get some exercise.

join (joins, joining, joined)

1. *vb.* When you *join* something, you put the two parts together to make one thing.
2. *vb.* If you *join* a group or a club, you become part of it.

joke (jokes, joking, joked)
1. *n.* A *joke* is a funny saying or story.
2. *vb.* If you *joke*, you fool about.

journey (journeys)
n. If you go on a *journey*, you travel from one place to another.

joy
n. Joy is a feeling of great happiness.

juice (juice or juices)
n. Juice is the liquid that comes out of fruit when you squeeze it.

a b c d e f g h i **j** k l m

jumble (jumbles, jumbling, jumbled)

1. *n.* A *jumble* is a mixture of all sorts of things.
2. *n.* A *jumble* sale is a sale to raise money for charity. People give all the things they don't want any more and other people buy them for small amounts of money.
3. *vb.* If you *jumble* things, you mix them together until they are all muddled up.

jump (jumps, jumping, jumped)

vb. When you *jump,* you move up and down suddenly into the air.

jumper (jumpers)

n. A *jumper* is a woolly top that you pull over your head to put on.

jungle (jungles)

n. A *jungle* is a forest in a hot country. The trees in a jungle are very tall and grow closely together.

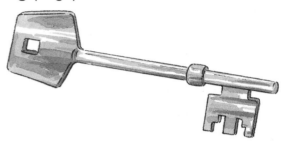

kale

n. *Kale* is a leafy, green vegetable.

keep (keeps, keeping, kept)

1. *vb.* If you *keep* something, you have it for yourself.
2. If you are told to '*Keep* off' or to '*Keep* away', from something, you must not go near it.

keeper (keepers)

n. A *keeper* is a person who looks after animals in a park or zoo, or who looks after a park.

kettle (kettles)

n. A *kettle* is a container with a lid that you use to boil water.

key (keys)

n. A *key* is a piece of metal that is specially shaped to fit in a lock, or to wind up clocks or toys.

kick (kicks, kicking, kicked)

vb. If you *kick* something like a ball, you hit it hard with your foot.

kidney (kidneys)

n. Your *kidneys* are the part of your body that keep your blood clean.

kid (kids)

1. *n.* A *kid* is a baby goat.
2. *n.* *Kid* is another name for a child.

kill (kills, killing, killed)

vb. If a person *kills*, they make an animal or person die.

killer (killers)

n. A *killer* is a person who has killed someone.

a b c d e f g h i j **k** l m

kilogram (kilograms)

n. A *kilogram* is a measurement of weight. It is equal to 1,000 grams.

kilometre (kilometres)

n. A *kilometre* is a measurement of distance. It is equal to 1,000 metres.

kind (kinder, kindest)

adj. A *kind* person is caring and loving to other people.

king (kings)

n. A *king* is the man who rules a country.

kingdom (kingdoms)

n. A *kingdom* is a country ruled over by a king or queen.

kiss (kisses, kissing, kissed)

vb. When you *kiss* someone, you touch them with your lips to show that you are very fond of them.

kitchen (kitchens)

n. A *kitchen* is a room in a house where food is prepared and cooked. The washing-up is also done in the kitchen.

kitten (kittens)

n. A *kitten* is a baby cat.

knead (kneads, kneading, kneaded)

vb. When you *knead* dough, you push and pull it to make it ready for baking into bread.

knee (knees)

n. Your *knee* is the joint in your leg. It is the place where your leg bends.

knew see **know**

knife (knives)

n. A *knife* is a tool with a blade that you use for cutting.

knit (knits, knitting, knitted)

vb. When you *knit,* you use wool and a pair of needles to make clothes like jumpers.

knob (knobs)

n. A *knob* is a round handle on a drawer or a door.

knock (knocks, knocking, knocked)

vb. When you *knock* something, you hit it or bump into it.

know (knows, knowing, knew, known)

vb. If you *know* something, you have something in your mind that you have found out or learnt. If many people know the same information, it is well-known.

a b c d e f g h i j **k l** m

ladder (ladders)

n. A *ladder* is made of two long poles with short bars between them so that you can climb up and down.

lady (ladies)

n. Lady is a polite name for a woman.

ladybird (ladybirds)

n. A *ladybird* is a small, red beetle with black spots.

lake (lakes)

n. A *lake* is an area of fresh water with land all around it.

lamb (lambs)

n. A *lamb* is a baby sheep.

land (lands, landing, landed)

1. *n. Land* is the part of the world that is not covered by sea. It is dry ground.
2. *vb.* If a boat or an aeroplane *lands*, it arrives.

lap (laps, lapping, lapped)

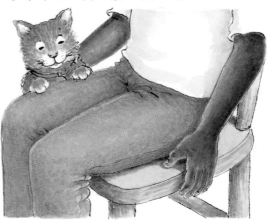

1. *n.* Your *lap* is the part of your body between your knees and hips when you are sitting down.
2. *vb.* If a cat *laps* milk, it drinks it using its tongue.

large (larger, largest)

adj. Something *large* is big.

larva (larvae)

n. A *larva* is an insect at a very early stage of its life.

last (lasts, lasting, lasted)
1. *vb.* If something *lasts*, it goes on for a long time.
2. *adj.* If you are *last,* everyone else is in front of you.

late (later, latest)
1. *adj.* If you are *late* getting to a place, you arrive after the time that you arranged to be there.
2. *adj.* If it is *late* in the day, the month or the year, it is near the end.

laugh (laughs, laughing, laughed)
vb. If you *laugh,* you make the sound that people make when they are happy or think something is funny.

lava

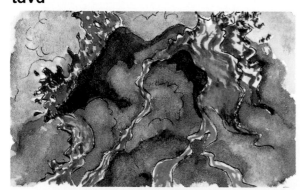

n. Lava is a kind of rock that comes from volcanoes. It is a red hot liquid at first and then it cools down and hardens.

law (laws)
n. A *law* is a rule made by the government.

lazy (lazier, laziest)

adj. Someone who is *lazy* does not want to do anything hard.

lead (leads, leading, led)
vb. If you *lead* someone to a place, you take them there to show them the way.

leader (leaders)
n. If you are the *leader* of a group of other people, you tell them what to do and where to go.

leaf (leaves)
n. A *leaf* is one of the thin, flat parts of a plant. *Leaves* are usually green.

leak (leaks, leaking, leaked)

vb. If something *leaks,* water, air or gas gets out through a small hole when it should not.

a b c d e f g h i j k l m

lean (leans, leaning, leaned or leant)

vb. If you *lean* against something, you rest your body against it.

leap (leaps, leaping, leapt)
vb. If you *leap,* you jump a long way.

learn (learns, learning, learned or learnt)
vb. When you *learn* about something, you find out about it or how to do it.

least
adj. The *least* of something is the smallest amount of it.

leave (leaves, leaving, left)
vb. If you *leave* something, you do not take it with you.

ledge (ledges)
n. A *ledge* is a narrow shelf on a window, wall or mountainside.

left
1. *adj.* Your *left* hand is the opposite to your right hand.
2. See *leave.*

leg (legs)
n. Your *legs* are the two long parts of your body that you use for walking.

lemonade
n. Lemonade is a drink made from the juice of lemons. It is usually fizzy and sweet.

length (lengths)
1. *n.* The *length* of something is the measurement of its longest side.
2. *n.* The *length* of time something takes, is how long it is from the start to the finish.

leopard (leopards)

n. A *leopard* is a big wild cat that has yellow fur with black spots on it.

less (lesser, least)
adj. Less means not as much as before.

lesson (lessons)
n. A *lesson* is a period of time when your teacher is teaching you.

letter (letters)
1. *n.* A *letter* is a message that someone writes to you and sends through the post.
2. B, H and V are *letters.* There are 26 letters in the alphabet.

n o p q r s t u v w x y z

lettuce (lettuces)

n. A *lettuce* is a salad vegetable.

levee (levees)

n. A *levee* is a high bank that is built along a river to stop it flooding.

level (levels)

1. *n.* The *level* of a liquid in a container, or the level of a lake or river, is how high up it is.
2. *adj.* If something is *level,* it is flat.

lever (levers)

1. *n.* A *lever* is a handle on a machine that you pull or push to make it work.

2. *n.* A *lever* is a strong bar that you put under something heavy so that you can lift it.

leveret (leverets)

n. A *leveret* is a baby hare.

lice see **louse**

licensed

adj. If you are *licensed* to do something, you have special official permission to do it.

lick (licks, licking, licked)

vb. If you *lick* something, you move your tongue across it to taste it, to make it wet or to clean it.

lid (lids)

n. A *lid* is the top of a box or container which can be taken off.

lie (lies, lying, lay, lain; lied)

1. *n.* A *lie* is something that you say that is not true.
2. *vb.* If you *lie* somewhere, you rest your body flat on something.
3. *vb.* When you *lie,* you do not tell the truth.

life (lives)

n. Life is being alive. Humans, plants and animals all have life.

lifts (lifts, lifting, lifted)

1. *n.* A *lift* is a machine that takes people up and down inside tall buildings.
2. *vb.* If you *lift* something, you move it upwards to a higher place.

light (lights, lighting, lighted, lit; lighter, lightest)

1. *n.* *Light* is the brightness that lets you see. Light comes from the sun, the moon, candles, fire and lamps.
2. *n.* A *light* is anything that gives you brightness in the dark and lets you see.
3. *vb.* If you *light* a fire, you make it burn.
4. *adj.* If something is *light*, it is not heavy.

lighthouse (lighthouses)

n. A *lighthouse* is a tower built near the coast or on a small island in the sea. It has a strong, flashing light at the top. The light flashes to guide ships or to warn them of danger.

lightning

n. *Lightning* is a very bright and sudden flash of light in the sky, which happens during a thunderstorm.

like (likes, liking, liked)

1. If you *like* something or someone, they make you happy.
2. *adj.* If two things are *like* each other, they are similar in some way.

limb (limbs)

n. Your *limbs* are your arms and your legs.

limpet (limpets)

n. A *limpet* is a shellfish that clings to rocks.

line (lines)

n. A *line* is a long, thin mark on a surface.

linen

1. *n.* *Linen* is a cloth made from a plant called flax.
2. *n.* *Linen* is all your sheets, tablecloths and towels.

link (links, linking, linked)
1. *n.* A *link* is a piece in a chain.
2. *vb.* If you *link* things, you join them together.

lion (lions)

n. A *lion* is a large animal with brownish, yellow fur which belongs to the cat family. A female lion is called a *lioness*.

lip (lips)

n. Your *lips* are the soft red parts at the edge of your mouth.

liquid (liquids)
n. *Liquid* is anything that can be poured, like milk or water.

list (lists)
n. A *list* is a set of things that you write down one after the other.

listen (listens, listening, listened)
vb. When you *listen,* you hear what someone else is saying and you pay attention to it.

litter
n. *Litter* is rubbish such as waste paper and empty bottles, that is left lying around.

little (littler, littlest)
adj. If something is *little*, it is very small.

live (lives, living, lived)
vb. If something *lives,* it is alive.

living see **live**

lizard (lizards)
n. A *lizard* is a small creature with four short legs and a long tail. *Lizards* are reptiles and have rough, dry skins.

load (loads, loading, loaded)
vb. If someone *loads* a vehicle, they put things in it to take them somewhere else.

loaf (loaves)
n. A *loaf* is bread that has been baked in one piece. *Loaves* can be sliced.

local (locals)
adj. *Local* means that things belong to a place. The local shops are the shops near to where you are.

lock (locks, locking, locked)
1. *n.* A *lock* is the part of a door that you use to keep it shut.

a b c d e f g h i j k l m

2. *vb.* If you *lock* a door, you use a key to close it so that no-one else can open it.

log (logs)

n. A *log* is a thick piece of a tree that has been cut down and chopped up.

lolly (lollies)

n. A *lolly* is a sweet or a flavoured ice, on a stick.

lonely (lonelier, loneliest)

adj. If you are *lonely*, you feel unhappy because you have no friends.

long (longer, longest)

1. *adj.* If something takes a *long* time, it takes a great deal of time.
2. *adj.* If a road is *long*, it is a great distance from one end to the other.

look (looks, looking, looked)

vb. If you *look* at something, you use your eyes to see what is there.

loop (loops)

n. A *loop* is a ring of something like wire, thread or ribbon.

loose (looser, loosest)

adj. If something is *loose*, it is not tight.

lord (lords)

1. *n.* A *lord* was a person, long ago, who owned large areas of land and had many people working for him.
2. *n.* Today, *Lord* is a special title people have if they are important in some way.

lorry (lorries)

n. A *lorry* is a large machine on wheels that carries heavy loads for long distances.

lose (loses, losing, lost)

1. *vb.* If you *lose* something, you cannot find it.

2. *adj.* If you are *lost*, you do not know where you are or cannot find the people you were with.

loud (louder, loudest)

adj. Something *loud* makes a lot of noise and is easy to hear.

louse (lice)

n. A *louse* is a small insect that lives on the bodies of people and animals and bites them to use their blood as food.

love (loves, loving, loved)

1. *n.* *Love* is a very strong feeling you have when you like someone very much.
2. *vb.* If you *love* someone or something, you like them very much.

lovely (lovelier, loveliest)

adj. Something *lovely* is beautiful to look at or listen to.

low (lower, lowest)

adj. Something that is *low*, is close to the ground.

lower (lowers, lowering, lowered)

vb. If you *lower* something, you slowly move it downwards.

luck

n. *Luck* is something good that happens without any reason to explain it.

lucky (luckier, luckiest)

adj. Someone who is *lucky* has good luck.

lullaby (lullabies)

n. A *lullaby* is a song for helping children to get to sleep at night time.

lump (lumps)

n. A *lump* is a piece of something solid, like a lump of wood or a sugar lump. If something like custard is lumpy, it is not smooth and has bits in it.

lunch (lunches)

n. *Lunch* is the meal that you have in the middle of the day.

lunch time (lunch times)

n. *Lunch time* is the time between morning and afternoon when you have a break to eat a meal.

lying see lie

a b c d e f g h i j k **l** **m**

M m

machine (machines)

n. A *machine* is something with several parts that work together to do a job. *Machines* usually work by electricity or have an engine. Cars, computers and cookers are machines.

machinery

n. Machinery is a collection of machines.

mad (madder, maddest)

adj. If someone is *mad*, they are very angry.

magic

n. Magic is the power to do wonderful things or tricks that people cannot usually do.

magical

adj. If you say that something is *magical*, it is very special and you can hardly believe it is true.

magpie (magpies)

n. A *magpie* is a black and white bird.

maid (maids)

n. A *maid* is a woman or a girl who is a servant.

mail

n. Mail is another name for the letters and parcels that the postman brings.

main

adj. Main means the most important. Main roads are important roads.

mainland

n. The *mainland* is the largest part of a country that has islands nearby.

majesty (majesties)

n. 'Your *Majesty*' is the polite way to speak to a king or queen.

major (majors)

1. *n.* A *major* is an important officer in the army.
2. *adj.* If something is *major*, it is more important than anything else.

make (makes, making, made)

1. *vb.* When you *make* something, you shape it or build it by putting things together.
2. If you *make* way for someone, you move out of their way to let them go past.

maker (makers)

n. The *maker* of something is the person who made it.

male (males)

n. A *male* is the person or animal who does not give birth to children.

mallard (mallards)

n. A *mallard* is a wild duck.

mammal (mammals)

n. A *mammal* is any warm-blooded animal that has a backbone and which feeds its babies on milk. Human beings, lions, bats and whales are all *mammals*.

man (men)

n. A *man* is a grown-up boy.

mane (manes)

n. A *mane* is the hair that grows on the neck of a horse, donkey or lion.

mango (mangoes)

n. A *mango* is a tree which has yellowish, sweet-tasting fruit. *Mangoes* grow in hot countries.

map (maps)

n. A *map* is a drawing of a place as it would look from above. It shows the shape of the land, the mountains and rivers, the towns, villages and cities and the roads and the railways.

a b c d e f g h i j k l m

marathon (marathons)

n. A *marathon* is a race where many people run a distance of about 26 miles or 42 kilometres.

march (marches, marching, marched)

vb. When you *march*, you walk with regular steps like a soldier.

mark (marks, marking, marked)

1. *n.* A *mark* is something on a surface that is a different colour to all the rest and should not be there.
2. *vb.* If you *mark* something, you make a patch of a different colour on it.
3. *vb.* If teachers *mark* your work, they look at it carefully and tell you what they think about it.

market (markets)

n. A *market* is a place, usually in the open air, where things are bought and sold at stalls.

marry (marries, marrying, married)

vb. If one person *marries* another, they become husband and wife.

marvellous

adj. If something is *marvellous*, it is wonderful and better than you expected it to be.

mask (masks)

n. A *mask* is a cover for your face.

mat (mats)

n. A *mat* is a small carpet.

match (matches, matching, matched)

1. *n.* A *match* is a sporting competition like a tennis match or a football match.
2. *n.* A *match* is a small stick of wood. One end is specially treated so that when you strike it hard against a matchbox, it catches fire and makes a flame.
3. *vb.* If you *match* two things, you find everything about them that is the same.

mate (mates)

1. *n.* *Mate* is a name for a sailor.
2. *n.* *Mates* are a pair of animals which have young together.

material (materials)

1. *n. Material* is another name for fabric or cloth.
2. *n. Materials* are anything you need to make something.

matter (matters, mattering, mattered)

1. *n. Matter* is what the world is made of.
2. If you say 'What is the *matter*?' you want to know what is wrong.

may

1. When you say that something *may* be true, you mean it could be true but you are not sure.
2. If you say '*May* I have one?', you are asking politely for something.

maybe

adv. Maybe means you are not certain about something.

mayor (mayors)

n. A *mayor* is a man who is chosen by a town to represent its people. A woman who does this is called a *mayoress*.

meadow (meadows)

n. A *meadow* is a large, grassy field.

meal (meals)

n. A *meal* is food people eat. Breakfast, lunch and supper are *meals*.

mean (means, meaning, meant; meaner, meanest)

1. *vb.* If you ask someone what they *mean,* you want something explained to you.
2. *adj.* If someone is *mean*, they are unkind and unpleasant.

meanwhile

adv. If something happens *meanwhile*, it happens at the same time as something else.

measure (measures, measuring, measured)

1. *n.* A *measure* is an amount of something.
2. *vb.* If you *measure* something, you find out how tall it is, how deep it is or how heavy it is.

a b c d e f g h i j k l m

meat (meats)

n. Meat is the flesh of animals that we eat.

mechanical

adj. Mechanical means things to do with machines.

medical

adj. Medical means things to do with people's health.

medicine (medicines)

n. Medicine is a liquid or tablets that the doctor gives you to make you feel better when you are ill.

medium

adj. Medium means not big and not small, but in between.

meet (meets, meeting, met)

vb. When people *meet*, they come to a place together and say hello.

melt (melts, melting, melted)

vb. If something *melts*, it changes from hard to soft because it has been heated.

men see **man**

mend (mends, mending, mended)

vb. If you *mend* something, you put it back together after it has been broken.

menu (menus)

n. A *menu* is a list of things in a café or restaurant that you can buy to eat.

mermaid (mermaids)

n. A *mermaid* is an imaginary creature that has a woman's body and a fish's tail and lives in the sea.

merry (merrier, merriest)

adj. If you are *merry*, you are happy, cheerful and bright.

mess (messes, messing, messed)

1. *n.* If things are in a *mess*, they are untidy.
2. *vb.* If you *mess* with things, you play about with them.

message (messages)

n. A *message* is words or information that you leave for someone when you cannot speak to them.

Walk past the fountain, turn right at the summerhouse. Take the left fork in the path to the Gazebo. M.

messy (messier, messiest)

adj. Something *messy* is not tidy. People who leave things lying around, or who spill things, are messy.

met see **meet**

metal (metals)

n. Metal is a hard material like iron, steel or silver.

meteorologist (meteorologists)

n. A *meteorologist* studies the weather.

metre (metres)

n. A *metre* is a measurement of length. It is equal to 100 centimetres.

mice see **mouse**

middle (middles)

n. The *middle* of something is halfway between the beginning and the end, or halfway between the top and the bottom.

mighty (mightier, mightiest)

adj. If a person is *mighty*, they are very strong.

mile (miles)

n. A *mile* is a measurement of distance. It is equal to 1.6 kilometres.

milk

1. *n. Milk* is a white liquid that comes from cows and goats. People can drink milk.
2. *n. Milk* is the white liquid that mothers use to feed their babies.

milkman (milkmen)

n. A *milkman* is a person whose job is to deliver milk to people's houses.

mill (mills)

n. A *mill* is a building where grain is crushed to make flour.

millipede (millipedes)

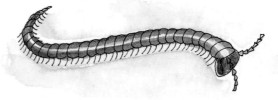

n. A *millipede* is a small, long creature with lots of legs.

mind (minds, minding, minded)

1. *vb.* If you *mind* about something, you care about it.
2. If you change your *mind*, you do not do what you were going to do in the first place.

a b c d e f g h i j k l **m**

mine (mines, mining, mined)

1. *n.* A *mine* is a place underground where people work to dig out coal, jewels, salt or metals.
2. If you say 'it is *mine*', you mean it belongs to you.

miner (miners)

n. A *miner* is a person who works underground to find coal, jewels, salt or metals.

mini-beast (mini-beasts)

n. A *mini-beast* is a small creature like an insect, beetle or spider.

minute (minutes)

n. One *minute* is a measure of time. It is 60 seconds. There are 60 *minutes* in one hour.

miracle (miracles)

n. A *miracle* is something marvellous which some people believe only God could have made happen.

mirror (mirrors)

n. A *mirror* is a flat piece of glass in which you can see yourself.

miss (misses, missing, missed)

1. *vb.* If you *miss* someone, you are sad that they are not with you.
2. *adj.* If someone is *missing*, they are not where they should be.
3. *Miss* is the polite way of writing or speaking to a woman who is not married. You say '*Miss* Jones' or '*Miss* Hayes'.

mite (mites)

n. A *mite* is a tiny creature.

mix (mixes, mixing, mixed)

vb. When you *mix* things, you put them together and stir or shake them.

mixture (mixtures)

n. A *mixture* is two or more things stirred up together.

moan (moans, moaning, moaned)

1. *vb.* If you *moan*, you make a low cry of pain or sadness.
2. *vb.* If you *moan* about something, you complain about it.

modern

adj. Modern means the kinds of things that are to do with life around you now.

mole (moles)

n. A *mole* is a small animal that lives underground. It has tiny eyes and short dark fur.

moment (moments)

n. A *moment* is a short amount of time.

money

n. Money is the coins and pieces of paper used by people when they buy and sell things.

monkey (monkeys)

n. A *monkey* is an animal with hands, feet and a long tail, that lives in trees in hot countries.

monster (monsters)

n. A *monster* is a huge, terrifying creature that you find in stories.

month (months)

n. A *month* is one of the twelve parts of the year.

moon (moons)

n. The *moon* is a round object in the sky, that shines at night. The moon goes round the earth once in every four weeks.

moonlight

n. Moonlight is the light from the moon.

moor (moors, mooring, moored)

1. *n.* A *moor* is open land with heather and grass growing on it.
2. *vb.* When you *moor* a boat, you tie it up.

a b c d e f g h i j k l m

morning (mornings)

n. Morning is the first part of the day from sunrise until lunch time.

mosque (mosques)

n. A *mosque* is a building where people of the Muslim faith go to worship.

mosquito (mosquitoes)

n. A *mosquito* is a small flying insect that sucks blood for its food.

moss (mosses)

n. Moss is a very small green plant that grows in damp places.

moth (moths)

n. A *moth* is an insect with large wings. *Moths* usually fly at night.

mother (mothers)

n. A *mother* is a woman with a child or children of her own.

motor (motors)

n. A *motor* is the part inside a machine that makes it work.

moult (moults, moulting, moulted)

vb. When an animal or bird *moults*, its old fur or feathers fall out and new fur or feathers grow.

mound (mounds)

n. A *mound* is a small hill.

mount (mounts, mounting, mounted)

vb. If you *mount* a horse, you get on to its back.

mountain (mountains)

n. A *mountain* is a very high hill. It is often steep and difficult to climb.

mouse (mice)

n. A *mouse* is a tiny animal with sharp teeth, whiskers and a long tail.

moustache (moustaches)

n. A *moustache* is the hair on a man's top lip.

mouth (mouths)

n. Your *mouth* is the opening that you put your food in so that you can eat it.

move (moves, moving, moved)

1. *vb.* When you *move,* you go from one place to another.
2. *vb.* When you *move* something, you take it from one place and put it in another.

movement (movements)

n. If you see or hear a *movement,* you notice someone or something moving.

movie (movies)

n. A *movie* is a film.

mud

n. *Mud* is a wet and sticky mixture of earth and water. If you walk or play in mud you get muddy.

mum (mums)

n. *Mum* or mummy is another way of saying mother.

mumble (mumbles, mumbling, mumbled)

vb. If you *mumble* you do not speak clearly.

munch (munches, munching, munched)

vb. If you *munch* something, you chew it noisily.

mushroom (mushrooms)

n. A *mushroom* is a type of fungus with a short thick stem and a round top. You can eat some *mushrooms* but others are poisonous.

a b c d e f g h i j k l m

music

    n. Music is made up of sounds that people sing or play on instruments.

mussel (mussels)

    n. A *mussel* is a shellfish that clings to rocks. Its shell has two halves and is blue-black in colour.

mustard

    n. Mustard is a hot spice.

mutter (mutters, muttering, muttered)

    vb. If you *mutter,* you talk quietly and quickly, so that you are difficult to hear.

mysterious

    adj. Mysterious means something is strange and cannot be explained.

mystery (mysteries)

    n. A *mystery* is something strange and puzzling that has happened.

name (names, naming, named)

1. *n.* Your *name* is what you are called.
2. *vb.* When you *name* someone or something, you give them a name.

nanny (nannies)

1. *n.* A *nanny* is a person whose job is to live with a family and look after the children.
2. *n.* A *nanny* is a female goat.
3. *n.* Nanny is another name for grandmother.

narrow (narrower, narrowest)

adj. Something that is *narrow*, is thin not wide.

nasty (nastier, nastiest)

adj. Someone or something *nasty*, is very unpleasant.

natal

adj. Natal means to do with the time of a birth.

national

adj. Something *national* belongs to the country and the people who live there.

near (nearer, nearest)

adj. If something or someone is *near* to a place, thing or person, it is only a short distance away.

nearly

adv. If you *nearly* do something, you almost do it, but not quite.

a b c d e f g h i j k l m

neat (neater, neatest)

adj. If something or someone is *neat*, they are tidy and clean.

neck (necks)

n. Your *neck* is the part of your body that joins your head to your shoulders.

necklace (necklaces)

n. A *necklace* is a piece of jewellery that you wear around your neck.

nectar

n. Nectar is the sweet liquid that bees collect from plants.

need (needs, needing, needed)

vb. If you *need* something, it is important that you have it.

needle (needles)

n. A *needle* is a metal object that you use for sewing. It is small, very thin and pointed at one end with a slot at the other to take thread.

neigh (neighs, neighing, neighed)

vb. When a horse *neighs*, it makes a loud noise through its nose.

neighbour (neighbours)

Your *neighbour* is the person who lives next door to you.

neighbourhood (neighbourhoods)

n. Your *neighbourhood* is the area around your home.

nest (nests, nesting, nested)

1. *n.* A *nest* is a warm home for a bird or other small animal.
2. *vb.* When an animal or bird *nests*, it makes a home for its young.

nestling (nestlings)

n. A *nestling* is a baby bird which is too young to fly and cannot leave the nest.

net (nets)

n. Fishermen use a *net* to catch fish.

nettle (nettles)

n. A *nettle* is a plant which has leaves that can sting.

never

adv. If you say *never*, you mean not at any time.

new (newer, newest)
1. *adv.* *New* things have just been bought or made.
2. *adv.* *New* things are different.

news

n. *News* is information about things that have just happened.

newspaper (newspapers)
n. A *newspaper* is lots of sheets of paper which are printed with information about everything that is going on in the world. *Newspapers* are sold everyday.

next
adj. If something happens *next*, it happens straight after what is happening now.

nibble (nibbles, nibbling, nibbled)
vb. If you *nibble* something, you take little bites of it.

nice (nicer, nicest)
adj. *Nice* means pleasant, kind or friendly.

night (nights)
n. *Night* is the time between sunset and sunrise when it is dark and most people, and many animals, are asleep.

nightdress (nightdresses)
n. A *nightdress* is a loose dress that girls and women wear in bed.

nightly
adv. If something happens *nightly*, it happens every night.

nobody (nobodies)
Nobody means not anyone.

nocturnal

adj. If an animal is *nocturnal*, it sleeps in the day and wakes up at night.

noise (noises)
n. A *noise* is a sound. It is often loud.

noisy (noisier, noisiest)
adj. If someone or something is *noisy*, they make a lot of sound.

a b c d e f g h i j k l m

nomad (nomads)

n. A *nomad* is one of a group of people who move from place to place.

north

n. North is one of the four main compass points.

northern

adj. Northern means in, or from, the North.

nose (noses)

n. You breathe and smell with your *nose*.

nostril (nostrils)

n. Your *nostrils* are the two openings at the end of your nose.

note (notes)

1. *n.* A *note* is a short message that you write.
2. *n.* A *note* is a single sound in music.

nothing

Nothing means not anything at all.

notice (notices, noticing, noticed)

1. *n.* A *notice* is a sign which gives you information.
2. *vb.* If you *notice* something or someone, you see or hear them and think about it.

now

adv. Something that happens *now*, happens at the present time.

nowhere

adv. Nowhere means not anywhere.

number (numbers, numbering, numbered)

1. *n.* A *number* tells you how many. Any of the words or figures used for counting are *numbers*.
2. *vb.* If you *number* objects, you give them each a number.

nurse (nurses)

n. A *nurse* is a person whose job is to look after you if you are hurt or ill and are in hospital.

nursery (nurseries)

1. *n.* A *nursery* is a place where young children are looked after and can play and learn together.

2. *n.* A *nursery* is a place where young plants and trees are grown.

nut (nuts)

1. *n.* A *nut* is the hard fruit of some trees which grows inside a hard shell.
2. *n.* A *nut* is a metal fastener which fits onto a bolt.

nutmeg (nutmegs)

n. *Nutmeg* is a spice made from the dried fruit of a tropical tree, which is grated or ground into a powder to flavour puddings and other foods.

nymph (nymphs)

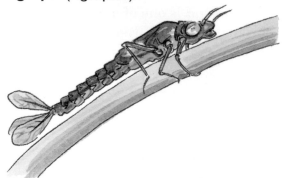

1. *n.* A *nymph* is the larva of an insect. It turns into an adult without changing into a pupa.
2. *n.* A *nymph* is a spirit of nature in fairy stories and in myths.

128   a b c d e f g h i j k l m

oak (oaks)

n. An *oak* is a large tree. It grows from an acorn and it loses its leaves in winter.

oasis (oases)

n. An *oasis* is a place in the desert where there is water and where trees and plants grow.

oat (oats)

n. *Oats* are the grains of a cereal plant grown by farmers. Oats can be used to make food like porridge.

ocean (oceans)

n. An *ocean* is one of the large areas of water on the earth's surface.

octogenarian (octogenarians)

n. An *octogenarian* is a person who is between 80 and 89 years old.

office (offices)

n. An *office* is a place where one person or several people work. *Offices* usually have lots of files,  papers and books in them with secretaries to keep them in order. A lot of business is done in offices.

officer (officers)

n. An *officer* is a person who is important in the army, navy or the police.

often

adv. If something happens *often*, it happens again and again.

oil (oils)

1. *n.* *Oil* is a thick, smooth liquid that is found underground. It is used to keep engines running smoothly.
2. *n.* Some *oil* is made from plants and can be used for cooking or for making dressings.
3. *n.* Some *oils* are used to rub onto your skin to protect you from the sun or to make your skin soft.

old (older, oldest)

adj. Someone or something that is *old*, has been around for a long time.

olive (olives)

n. An *olive* is a small, green or black fruit with a stone in the centre. *Olives* are pressed to make olive oil. They can also be used in cooking or eaten as a snack.

once

adv. If something happens *once*, it happens one time only.

only

adj. If you are the *only* person, there is no-one else.

ooze (oozes, oozing, oozed)

vb. If something such as a liquid *oozes*, it flows very slowly.

open (opens, opening, opened)

1. *vb.* If you *open* something like a box, you take off the lid.
2. *vb.* If you *open* a door, you move it so that you can go through.
3. *vb.* If something like a seed *opens*, it breaks apart.
4. *adj.* If something is *open*, it is not shut.

orange (oranges)

n. An *orange* is a round, juicy fruit that grows in hot countries.

order (orders, ordering, ordered)

1. *n.* If a shopkeeper has an *order*, he or she has to get something for a customer.
2. *n.* If you give an *order*, you tell someone to do something.
3. *vb.* If you *order* something from a shop, you ask them to get it for you.

ordinary

adj. *Ordinary* things are not unusual. You can see ordinary things all the time.

a b c d e f g h i j k l m

other (others)

1. *adj. Other* things are things that are different.
2. *adj.* If you say something happened the *other* day, you mean it happened a few days ago.

otter (otters)

n. An *otter* is a rare animal that lives near water. It has short brown fur, a long tail and webbed feet. *Otters* can swim and live on fish and other small animals.

out

1. *adv. Out* is not in.
2. *adv.* If you go *out* of a place, you are not there any more.
3. *adv.* If a fire is *out*, it is not burning any more.

outside (outsides)

1. *n.* The *outside* of something is the surface or the edges of it.
2. *adv.* If you are *outside*, you are in the open air.

oven (ovens)

n. An *oven* is the box-shaped part of a cooker where you put food to roast or bake.

owl (owls)

n. An *owl* is a bird that hunts at night. It has a flat face and large eyes.

owns (owns, owning, owned)

1. *vb.* If you *own* something, it belongs to you.
2. If you are on your *own*, there is no-one else with you.

owner (owners)

n. If you are the *owner* of something, it belongs to you.

oyster (oysters)

n. An *oyster* is a shellfish. Some *oysters* can be eaten and others are used for growing pearls.

P p

pace (paces, pacing, paced)

1. *n.* A *pace* is one walking step.
2. *n.* Your *pace* is your walking or your running speed.
3. *vb.* If you *pace*, you walk up and down because you are worried about something.

pack (packs, packing, packed)

1. *n.* A *pack* is a group of something, like a pack of cubs or a pack of dogs.
2. *vb.* If you *pack* something like a box or a suitcase, you put things into it to take somewhere else.

packet (packets)

n. A *packet* is a small parcel or container.

paddle (paddles, paddling, paddled)

1. *n.* A *paddle* is a pole with a flat blade at one or both ends. You use *paddles* to make boats move through water.
2. *vb.* If you *paddle*, you stand in shallow water with bare feet.

page (pages)

n. A *page* is one side of a piece of paper in a book or on a pad.

pail (pails)

n. A *pail* is a bucket.

pain (pains)

n. A *pain* is the sharp, unpleasant feeling you have if you are hurt or ill.

paint (paints, painting, painted)

1. *n.* *Paint* is a coloured liquid that is put on a surface with a brush or a roller.

a b c d e f g h i j k l m

2. *vb.* If you *paint* something, you use a brush, a roller or your hands to put coloured liquid on it.

pair (pairs)
   n. A *pair* of things is two of them that belong together, like a pair of scissors or a pair of shoes.

palace (palaces)

   n. A *palace* is a very large, important house where a royal family or a president lives.

pale (paler, palest)
   adj. Something that is *pale*, is light in colour.

palette (palettes)
   n. A *palette* is a board that an artist uses to mix paints.

pan (pans)
   n. A *pan* is a wide pot for cooking.

pane (panes)
   n. A *pane* is a sheet of glass in a window or a door.

pangolin (pangolins)

   n. A *pangolin* is a mammal that lives in Africa, Asia and Indonesia. Its body is covered with horny scales. It has a long nose for poking into ants' nests to find ants to eat.

panic (panics, panicking, panicked)
   1. *n.* Panic is a feeling of fear that makes you do things without thinking clearly.
   2. *vb.* If you *panic*, you stop thinking sensibly and do things in a frightened way.

pant (pants, panting, panted)
   vb. If you *pant*, you take very short, quick, shallow breaths.

paper (papers)
   1. *n.* Paper is the material that you write on, wrap things with, stick to things and paint on.
   2. *n.* A *paper* is another name for a newspaper.

parade (parades)

n. A *parade* is a procession of people on a special occasion or for an inspection.

parcel (parcels)

n. A *parcel* is something wrapped up in paper, ready to be posted or given as a present.

parent (parents)

n. A *parent* is a mother or a father.

park (parks)

1. *n.* A *park* is an open space in a town where people can go to walk, sit or play and enjoy themselves.
2. *vb.* When you *park* a car, you find a place where you can leave it for a while.

parrot (parrots)

n. A *parrot* is a tropical bird, which often has brightly coloured feathers.

part (parts, parting, parted)

1. *n.* A *part* of something is a piece that belongs to something bigger.
2. *n.* A *part* in a play is the character that you are.
3. *vb.* If you *part* things you divide them.

particular

adj. If you talk about someone or something in *particular*, you mean that person or thing only.

party (parties)

n. When you have a *party*, you ask your friends to come and share a special occasion with you.

pass (passes, passing, passed)

1. *vb.* When you *pass* someone or something, you go by.
2. *vb.* If you *pass* a test, you are successful in it.
3. *vb.* If you *pass* a ball to another player in a game, you give it to them.

a b c d e f g h i j k l m

passenger (passengers)

n. A *passenger* is anyone who travels on a train, in a boat or aeroplane or in a car. The driver is not a passenger.

past

n. The *past* is time gone by.

pasta

n. *Pasta* is a food made from a mixture of flour, eggs and water and then made into different shapes. Pasta is usually served with a delicious sauce.

pastry (pastries)

n. *Pastry* is a mixture of flour, water and fat. It can be rolled out flat and used to make pies and tarts.

pat (pats, patting, patted)

vb. If you *pat* someone or something, you tap them lightly with your fingers.

patch (patches)

1. *n.* A *patch* is a small area of something. It could be a patch of land, a patch of colour or a patch of cloud.
2. *n.* A *patch* is a piece of material that is used to cover a hole in something.

path (paths)

n. A *path* is a narrow way through somewhere.

patient (patients)

n. A *patient* is a person who is being looked after by a doctor.

patrol (patrols, patrolling, patrolled)

1. *n.* A *patrol* is a group of people, like the police or soldiers, who walk around an area to see what is going on there.
2. *vb.* When a group of people, like the police, *patrol* an area they walk around it to see that there is no danger.

pattern (patterns)

n. A *pattern* is lines or shapes that have been drawn over and over again.

pause (pauses, pausing, paused)

1. *n.* A *pause* is a short break in something you are doing or are saying.
2. *vb.* If you *pause*, you stop for a very short time.

pavement (pavements)

n. A *pavement* is a path which is a little higher than the road, where you can walk safely away from the traffic.

paw (paws)

n. A *paw* is the foot of an animal. It has soft pads underneath and claws for gripping.

pay (pays, paying, paid)

vb. When a person *pays* someone, they give them money in return for work or for something that they are buying.

pea (peas)

n. A *pea* is a small round seed which grows in a pod. *Peas* are eaten as vegetables.

peace

n. *Peace* is a feeling of quiet and calm.

peaceful

adj. A time or place that is *peaceful*, is quiet.

peacefully

adv. If you do something *peacefully*, you do it in a quiet, gentle way.

peacock (peacocks)

n. A *peacock* is a large male bird with long, brightly coloured tail feathers which it can spread into a fan shape. The female bird is called a *peahen*.

a b c d e f g h i j k l m

peak (peaks)

n. The *peak* of something is its highest point. The peak of a mountain is the top.

pear (pears)

n. A *pear* is a fruit with juicy white flesh. It is oval in shape and has a green or yellow skin.

pearl (pearls)

n. A *pearl* is a hard, shiny, white ball that grows inside an oyster shell. *Pearls* are made into jewellery.

peat

n. *Peat* is decayed plants which have been pressed down in the ground. It is dug out in squares and can be used as fuel, or for compost in the garden.

peck (pecks, pecking, pecked)

vb. When a bird *pecks* at seed, it picks it up with its beak in short, sharp movements.

peculiar

adj. If something is *peculiar*, it is strange or different.

pedal (pedals)

n. A *pedal* is the part of something that you press with your foot to make it work. A bicycle has *pedals*.

peel (peels, peeling, peeled)

1. *n.* *Peel* is the skin of fruits like bananas, apples and oranges.
2. *vb.* When you *peel* something, you take the skin off it.

peep (peeps, peeping, peeped)

vb. When you *peep* at something, you take a quick look.

peer (peers, peering, peered)

vb. If you *peer* at something, you look at it closely.

pellet (pellets)

n. A *pellet* is a small ball of something.

pen (pens)

n. A *pen* is a tool you use for writing in ink. You can get ball point *pens*, fountain pens or felt tip pens.

penalty (penalties)

n. A *penalty* is a punishment for something you do wrong.

pencil (pencils)
n. You use a *pencil* for writing or drawing. It is a thin wooden stick with a piece of graphite in the middle of it.

penguin (penguins)

n. A *penguin* is a black and white bird that cannot fly. It uses its wings for swimming. *Penguins* are from the Antarctic.

people
n. Men, women and children are all *people.*

pepper (peppers)
1. *n. Pepper* is a hot spice made into a powder that you can add to food.
2. *n.* A *pepper* is a red, green or yellow vegetable which can be eaten raw or cooked.

perch (perches)
n. A *perch* is a seat for a bird.

perfect
adj. Something which is *perfect,* has no faults.

perfectly
adv. If you do something *perfectly,* you do it so well that you could not do it better.

perform (performs, performing, performed)
vb. When you *perform,* you do something, like a dance, in front of a group of people.

perhaps
Perhaps means maybe or possibly.

person (persons)
n. A *person* is a man, a woman or a child.

pest (pests)
n. A *pest* is any person, or animal that causes a great deal of trouble.

pet (pets)

n. A *pet* is an animal that you like and keep in your home.

petal (petals)
n. A *petal* is one of the coloured parts of a flower.

a b c d e f g h i j k l m

petrol

n. *Petrol* is a liquid made from oil. You use petrol as a fuel for motors. Petrol makes cars move.

pet shop (pet shops)

n. A *pet shop* is a place where you can buy a pet.

phone (phones, phoning, phoned)

1. n. *Phone* is short for telephone. It is an instrument that you can use to speak to people who are in a different place or a long way away.
2. vb. If you *phone* someone, you use the telephone to speak to them when they are somewhere else.

photograph (photographs)

n. A *photograph* is a picture of someone or something that you take with a camera, using film.

piano (pianos)

n. A *piano* is a large musical instrument that has a row of black and white keys. The keys strike strings inside the piano when you press them. Each key makes a different sound.

piccolo (piccolos)

n. A *piccolo* is a small wind instrument that you play like a flute.

pick (picks, picking, picked)

1. vb. If you *pick* one thing, you choose it from several other things.
2. vb. If you *pick* fruit or flowers, you break them off and collect them.

pickle (pickles)

n. *Pickle* is a spicy mixture of vegetables and fruit which have been kept in vinegar for a long time. Pickle tastes strong and sharp.

picture (pictures)

n. A *picture* is a drawing, painting or photograph.

pie (pies)

n. A *pie* is a pastry case filled with things like meat, vegetables or fruit.

piece (pieces)

n. A *piece* of something is a bit of it.

pig (pigs)

n. A *pig* is a farm animal. It has thick skin and a curly tail. *Pigs* are usually rather fat.

pigeon (pigeons)

n. A *pigeon* is a bird, usually grey in colour, with a small head and a fat body. *Pigeons* make a soft cooing sound.

pile (piles, piling, piled)

1. *n.* A *pile* of something is a heap of it or many things built up on top of one another.
2. *vb.* If you *pile* things up, you put them on top of each other.

pilot (pilots)

n. A *pilot* is a person who controls a boat or an aeroplane.

pin (pins, pinning, pinned)

1. *n.* A *pin* is a small, sharp, metal object with a point at one end and a head at the other. *Pins* are used to hold things together.

2. *vb.* If you *pin* things together, you fasten them with a pin.

pincer (pincers)

n. A *pincer* is the sharp, curved claw of a crab or an insect.

pinch (pinches, pinching, pinched)

1. *n.* A *pinch* of something is the amount of it that you can hold between your finger and your thumb.
2. *vb.* If you *pinch* someone, you take a bit of their skin between your finger and thumb and squeeze it hard.

pine (pines)

n. A *pine* is a tall evergreen tree with very long, thin leaves called needles.

pineapple (pineapples)

n. A *pineapple* is a large fruit that grows in hot countries. It is sweet and juicy.

pink (pinker, pinkest)

adj. Something that is *pink*, is the colour between red and white.

pip (pips)

n. A *pip* is the seed of a fruit like an apple or a lemon.

a b c d e f g h i j k l m

pipe (pipes)

1. *n.* A *pipe* is a long, hollow tube that can be used to carry water, oil or other liquids from one place to another.
2. *n.* A *pipe* is a short, hollow tube with a bowl at the end that some people use to smoke tobacco.
3. *n.* A *pipe* is a musical instrument.

piper (pipers)

n. A *piper* is a person who plays music on a pipe.

pirate (pirates)

n. A *pirate* is a robber who steals from ships at sea.

pit (pits)

1. *n.* A *pit* is a large hole in the ground.
2. *n.* A *pit* is a coal mine. The opening to a pit is called the pithead.

pizza (pizzas)

n. A *pizza* is a flat, round piece of dough which is covered with tomatoes, cheese and other things and then baked in a very hot oven.

place (places, placing, placed)

1. *n.* A *place* is a particular area, spot or position.
2. *vb.* If you *place* something, you put it carefully onto a particular spot.

plain (plainer, plainest)

1. *n.* A *plain* is a large, flat area of land with very few trees on it.
2. *adj.* If something is *plain*, it is one colour and has no pattern on it.

plan (plans, planning, planned)

1. *n.* A *plan* is a drawing that shows what something looks like from above.
2. *vb.* If you *plan* what you are going to do, you decide before you do it.

plane (planes)

1. *n.* A *plane* is a tool for making wood smooth.
2. *n. Plane* is short for aeroplane.

plank (planks)

  n. A *plank* is a long, flat piece of wood.

plant (plants, planting, planted)

  1. *n.* A *plant* is a living thing that grows in the ground.

  2. *vb.* If you *plant* something, you put the seed, bulb or root into the ground so that it will grow.

plaster (plasters)

  1. *n.* A *plaster* is a covering for a small cut or graze.
  2. *n. Plaster* is a thick paste that hardens. You use plaster to cover a wall.

plastic (plastics)

  n. Plastic is a man-made material. It is very light and not easy to break. It can be used for making many different things.

plate (plates)

  n. A *plate* is a flat, round dish for serving and eating food.

platform (platforms)

  1. *n.* A *platform* in a hall is an area that is higher than all the rest.

  2. *n.* A railway *platform* is the place where people wait to get on and off trains.

play (plays, playing, played)

  1. *n.* A *play* is a story that you act out. Sometimes you can use puppets to act the parts.
  2. *vb.* When you *play*, you are in a game.

playground (playgrounds)

  n. A *playground* is a piece of land where children can play.

playtime (playtimes)

  n. Playtime is the time between lessons at school when you can play outside, or inside if it's raining.

pleasant (pleasanter, pleasantest)

  adj. Something that is *pleasant* is nice to listen to or to look at.

please (pleases, pleasing, pleased)

  1. *vb.* If you *please* someone, you make them happy.
  2. If you say 'please', you ask for something politely.

plenty

n. If you have *plenty* of something, you have more than enough.

plough (ploughs, ploughing, ploughed)

1. *n.* A *plough* is a farm machine that the farmer uses to turn over the earth before he plants the seeds for crops.
2. *vb.* If a farmer *ploughs* a field, he uses a machine to break up the earth.

pluck (plucks, plucking, plucked)

vb. If you *pluck* a stringed instrument, you use your fingers to pull the strings and make a sound.

plug (plugs)

1. *n.* You use a *plug* to connect electricity from the supply to the object that you want to use.
2. *n.* A *plug* is a piece of rubber used to block the hole in a sink or bath when full of water.

plumage

n. *Plumage* is the feathery covering on a bird.

plump (plumper, plumpest)

adj. A *plump* person or object is rather fat or large.

poacher (poachers)

n. A *poacher* is a person who catches fish, rabbits and game on other people's land without permission.

pocket (pockets)

n. A *pocket* is like a bag sewn into your clothes. You use a pocket to carry small things like money or a handkerchief.

poem (poems or poetry)

n. A *poem* is a piece of writing which is usually arranged in short lines and which often has a special pattern of rhyme or rhythm.

pod (pods)

n. A *pod* is a case for seeds that grows on some plants. Peas and beans grow in *pods*.

point (points, pointing, pointed)
1. *n.* A *point* is the sharp end of something.
2. *n.* A *point* is a mark that you score in a game.
3. *vb.* If you *point* at something, you show where it is by holding out your finger so that people look in the direction of something.

poison (poisons)
n. Poison is a liquid, powder or plant that can kill people and animals if they swallow it.

poke (pokes, poking, poked)
vb. If you *poke* someone, you push them hard with your finger or a stick.

polar
adj. Polar means to do with the North or the South pole.

pole (poles)
1. *n.* A *pole* is a long, strong stick of wood or metal.
2. *n.* The *poles* are the farthest points to the North and South on earth.

police
n. The *police* are the men and women who help to keep the laws of the country.

polish (polishes, polishing, polished)
1. *n.* You use *polish* to make things shine. There are different kinds of polish, like nail polish or furniture polish.
2. *vb.* When you *polish* something, you rub it with a cloth to make it shine.

pollen
n. Pollen is the fine powder that you find in flowers. It helps make seeds grow.

pollute (pollutes, polluting, polluted)
vb. If you *pollute* something, you spoil it by making it dirty or dangerous.

pollution

n. Pollution is all the unpleasant things that make water, air and everything around us dirty.

polo
n. Polo is a game like hockey that two teams of people play on horseback.

a   b   c   d   e   f   g   h   i   j   k   l   m

pond (ponds)

n. A *pond* is a small lake.

pony (ponies)

n. A *pony* is a small horse.

pool (pools)

n. A *pool* is a small area of quiet water.

poor (poorer, poorest)

adj. People who are *poor* do not have much money.

pop (pops, popping. popped)

vb. If something *pops*, it makes a sudden explosive sound.

poppy (poppies)

n. A *poppy* is a bright red flower which grows in meadows and cornfields.

popular

adj. *Popular* things or people are liked by everyone.

porpoise (porpoises)

n. A *porpoise* is a sea mammal, like a dolphin but smaller.

porridge

n. *Porridge* is a food made from oats with water and salt, or milk and sugar. It is usually eaten hot.

port (ports)

n. A *port* is a safe place for ships and boats to load and unload.

portcullis (portcullises)

n. A *portcullis* is a strong gateway made of bars that was used to defend castles and forts in times gone by.

post (posts, posting, posted)

1. *n.* *Post* is letters and parcels that the postman or postwoman delivers.
2. *n.* A *post* is a strong pole fixed in the ground.
3. *vb.* If you *post* a letter or a parcel, you put it in a post-box.

postcode (postcodes)

n. Your *postcode* is the group of letters and numbers that you put at the end of your address to show the area you live in.

poster (posters)

n. A *poster* is a large notice for people to read.

postman (postmen)

n. A *postman* is a person whose job is to deliver letters and parcels to you.

pot (pots)

n. A *pot* is a round container like a teapot, a flower pot or a jam pot.

potato (potatoes)

n. A *potato* is a root vegetable that grows under the ground. You cook it by boiling, frying or baking.

pounce (pounces, pouncing, pounced)

vb. If a cat *pounces* on a mouse, it leaps into the air and lands on it.

pound (pounds, pounding, pounded)

1. *n.* A *pound* is an amount of money.
2. *n.* A *pound* is a measure of weight equal to 0.454 kilograms.
3. *vb.* If you *pound* something, you crush it by beating it with something hard.

pour (pours, pouring, poured)

1. *vb.* If you *pour* a liquid, you tip it out of a container.
2. *vb.* If the rain *pours*, it falls very heavily.

powder (powders)

n. *Powder* is very small pieces of something. It is so fine that it looks like dust.

power (powers)

1. *n.* *Power* is control.
2. *n.* *Power* is being able to do something.
3. *n.* *Power* is physical strength.

practice (practices)

n. If you have a *practice*, like a cricket practice or a guitar practice, you do something over and over again to get better at it.

a b c d e f g h i j k l m

practise (practises, practising, practised)
vb. If you *practise* something, you do it over and over again to get better at it.

pram (prams)
n. A *pram* is a baby's cot on wheels.

prawn (prawns)
n. A *prawn* is an edible shellfish like a large shrimp.

pray (prays, praying, prayed)
vb. If you *pray*, you talk to God by saying a prayer.

preen (preens, preening, preened)
vb. Animals or people *preen* when they groom themselves.

present (presents, presenting, presented)

1. *n.* A *present* is something you are given to celebrate a special occasion, like a birthday.
2. *vb.* If you *present* someone with something, you give it to them.

press (presses, pressing, pressed)
vb. When you *press* something, you put weight on it.

pressure (pressures)
n. Pressure is the force you use when you press hard on something.

pretend (pretends, pretending, pretended)
vb. If you *pretend,* you make out that something is real or true when it is not.

pretty (prettier, prettiest)
adj. Pretty things or people are pleasing to look at.

prey

n. The *prey* of an animal or bird is the creatures that it hunts for food.

price (prices)
n. The *price* of something is how much money you must give to buy it.

prickly (pricklier, prickliest)
adj. Something that is *prickly,* has sharp spikes on it.

pride (prides)

1. *n. Pride* is a feeling of being happy and satisfied about what you are, what you do, how you look or about something you have done well.

2. *n.* A *pride* of lions is a group of lions that live together.

prince (princes)

n. A *prince* is the son of a king or queen.

princess (princesses)

n. A *princess* is the daughter of a king or queen.

print (prints, printing, printed)

1. *vb.* When someone *prints* a poster, a newspaper or a book, they use a machine to do the writing so that they can make lots of copies.

2. *vb.* If someone *prints* a pattern or a picture on a tee-shirt they use a machine to do it.

prize (prizes)

n. A *prize* is something that you are given as a reward for being very good at something.

problem (problems)

n. A *problem* is a difficulty that you have to sort out.

promise (promises, promising, promised)

vb. If you *promise* to do something, you say you will definitely do it.

properly

adv. If you do something *properly*, you do it in the right way.

protect (protects, protecting, protected)

vb. When you *protect* someone or something, you look after them and make sure that they come to no harm.

protein (proteins)

n. Protein is an important part of food which helps your body to grow.

proud (prouder, proudest)

adj. If you are *proud*, you are very pleased because you have done something very well.

a b c d e f g h i j k l m

prove (proves, proving, proved)

vb. When you *prove* something, you show that it is true.

provide (provides, providing, provided)

vb. When you *provide* something for someone, you make sure it is there if they need it.

pub (pubs)

n. A *pub* is a place where grown-ups can meet for a drink and something to eat. Pub is short for public house.

public

adj. If something is *public*, it is meant for everyone to use.

puddle (puddles)

n. A *puddle* is a very small pool of water.

puff (puffs, puffing, puffed)

1. *n.* A *puff* of air or smoke is a short burst of it.
2. *vb.* If you *puff*, you are out of breath and breathe in short, sharp bursts.

puffin (puffins)

n. A *puffin* is a black and white sea bird with a colourful beak.

pull (pulls, pulling, pulled)

vb. When you *pull* something, you get hold of it and make it come towards you.

pump (pumps, pumping, pumped)

1. *n.* A *pump* is a machine that forces air, gas or liquid out of or into something.
2. *vb.* If you *pump* something, you use a machine to force the air, gas or liquid into or out of it.

pumpkin (pumpkins)

n. A *pumpkin* is a large yellow fruit which is good for making lanterns with or for eating in pies.

puncture (punctures)

n. A *puncture* is a hole in something filled with air.

pupa (pupae)

n. A *pupa* is an insect in the stage between being an larva and an adult.

puppet (puppets)

n. A *puppet* is a kind of doll that you can move by using strings, rods or your hands.

puppy (puppies)

n. A *puppy* is a baby dog.

pure (pure, purer, purest)

adj. Something *pure* is clean and has nothing mixed with it.

purple (purpler, purplest)

adj. Something that is *purple,* is the colour of some grapes and plums. You can make purple by mixing red and blue together.

push (pushes, pushing, pushed)

vb. You *push* something when you press hard against it.

puzzle (puzzles)

n. A *puzzle* is a game or a question that is difficult to work out. You must concentrate hard to find the answer.

pyjamas

n. *Pyjamas* are the loose shirt and trousers that some people wear to sleep in.

python (pythons)

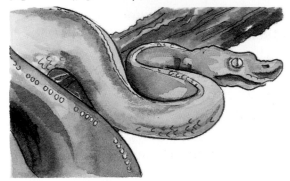

n. A *python* is a large snake that kills its prey by squeezing it.

a b c d e f g h i j k l m

QUACK!

quack (quacks, quacking, quacked)
1. *n.* A *quack* is the sound that a duck makes.
2. *vb.* When a duck makes a sound, it *quacks*.

quarter (quarters)

n. A *quarter* of something is one of four equal parts.

queen (queens)

1. *n.* A *queen* is the female ruler of a country.
2. *n.* A *queen* is the wife of a king.

quick (quicker, quickest)
adj. If you are *quick*, you can move very fast.

quiet (quieter, quietest)

adj. If you are *quiet*, you do not make much sound.

quite
1. *adv.* If you are *quite* sure about something, you are completely sure.
2. *adv.* If someone is *quite* likely to do something, they will probably do it.

rabbit (rabbits)

   n. A *rabbit* is a small furry animal with long ears and a small white tail. *Rabbits* can hop very fast on their strong back legs. They live in tunnels called burrows. All the burrows together are called a warren.

race (races, racing, raced)

   1. *n.* A *race* is a competition to see who is the fastest.

   2. *vb.* If you *race*, you go as fast as you can to try to be the fastest.

racehorse (racehorses)

   n. A *racehorse* is a horse which has been specially bred to run very fast.

rack (racks)

   n. A *rack* is a shelf made of open bars where you can put things like plates.

radiator (radiators)

   n. A *radiator* is a metal heater for a room.

raffle (raffles, raffling, raffled)

   1. *n.* A *raffle* is a way of raising money by selling tickets which have numbers on them. Numbers are picked out to see who wins the prize.

   2. *vb.* If you *raffle* something, you sell numbered tickets to people who want to win a prize.

raft (rafts)

   n. A *raft* is a flat platform that floats. It can be made of pieces of wood fixed together and can be used as a boat.

rag (rags)

   n. A *rag* is an old piece of cloth.

rail (rails)

> *n.* A *rail* is a bar or a rod, usually made of metal.

railway (railways)

> *n.* A *railway* is a way of carrying people or things from one place to another by train. The trains run on rails which are fixed to a track.

rain (rains, raining, rained)

> 1. *n.* Rain is the water that falls from the sky.
> 2. *vb.* When it *rains*, little drops of water fall from the sky. If it rains heavily, there is a rainstorm.

rainbow (rainbows)

> *n.* A *rainbow* is an arch of colours in the sky that you sometimes see when the sun shines through rain.

rainforest (rainforests)

> *n.* A *rainforest* is a thick forest of tall trees which grow in tropical countries where there is a lot of rain.

raise (raises, raising, raised)

> *vb.* If you *raise* something, you lift it up.

rake (raking, raked)

> 1. *n.* A *rake* is a garden tool with a long handle and spikes at the end for using in the garden.

> 2. *vb.* If you *rake* things such as leaves, you move them together using a rake.

ran see **run**

rang see **ring**

ranger (rangers)

> *n.* A *ranger* is a person who looks after parks or forests as a job.

rare (rarer, rarest)

> *adj.* If something is *rare*, it is unusual and not easy to find.

rat (rats)

> *n.* A *rat* is a small animal with long, sharp teeth. It has a long, scaly tail and looks like a large mouse.

rattle (rattles, rattling, rattled)

1. *n.* A *rattle* is a toy for a baby that makes a noise when it is shaken.
2. *vb.* If something *rattles*, it makes short, quick, knocking sounds.

raucous

adj. Raucous sounds are unpleasant and very loud.

ray (rays)

n. A *ray* is a thin band of light.

razor (razors)

n. A *razor* is a tool that people use to remove hair from their skin.

reach (reaches, reaching, reached)

vb. If you *reach* a place, you get there.

read (reads, reading, read)

vb. When you *read* something, you are able to see and understand words that are written down.

real

adj. Real things are things that exist and are not imagined.

realise (realises, realising, realised)

vb. When you *realise* something, you suddenly understand it clearly.

really

Really means truly.

receive (receives, receiving, received)

vb. If you *receive* something, it is given to you.

recipe (recipes)

n. A *recipe* is a list of instructions and ingredients that you need to make a meal.

recognise (recognises, recognising, recognised)

vb. If you *recognise* someone or something, you know who they are because you have seen them before.

record (records, recording, recorded)

1. *n.* A *record* is a disc of plastic that has music recorded on it.
2. *n.* A *record* is the best performance that someone can achieve.
3. *n.* A *record* is information about something that has happened that is written down.
4. *vb.* If you *record* something, you put sounds on tape or words on paper so that the information can be kept.

a b c d e f g h i j k l m

recorder (recorders)

n. A *recorder* is a musical instrument that you play by blowing through it. You make different notes by blocking off holes with your fingers.

red (redder, reddest)
adj. Something that is *red*, is the colour of ripe tomatoes.

reduce (reduces, reducing, reduced)
vb. If you *reduce* something, you make it smaller.

reel (reels)
n. A *reel* is an object that you wind string or wire around.

refer (refers, referring, referred)
vb. When you *refer* to someone or something, you mention them when you are speaking or writing.

reference
adj. A *reference* book is a book that you use for finding information.

reflection (reflections)
n. Your *reflection* is what you see when you look in a mirror or a shiny surface.

refrain (refrains, refraining, refrained)
1 *n.* A *refrain* is the chorus of a song that you sing after each verse.
2. *vb.* If you *refrain* from doing something, you don't do it.

refuse (refuses, refusing, refused)
vb. If you *refuse* to do something, you will not do it.

rein (reins)

n. A *rein* is one of a pair of leather straps that you use to control a horse.

related
adj. If you are *related* to somebody, you are part of their family.

relative (relatives)
n. Your *relatives* are all of your family, from your parents to your uncles and cousins and aunts.

religion (religions)

n. *Religion* is the way people believe in God and the way they worship.

remain (remains, remaining, remained)

vb. If something or somebody *remains*, they are still there when everything or everyone else has gone.

remember (remembers, remembering, remembered)

vb. When you *remember* something, you keep it in your mind.

remove (removes, removing, removed)

vb. If you *remove* something, you take it away.

repair (repairs, repairing, repaired)

vb. If you *repair* something, you fix it after it has been broken.

reply (replies, replying, replied)

vb. If you *reply*, you answer when someone speaks to you or writes to you.

reptile (reptiles)

n. A *reptile* is a cold-blooded creature with a scaly skin. The females lay eggs. Tortoises, lizards and snakes are *reptiles*.

rescue (rescues, rescuing, rescued)

vb. If a person *rescues* someone, they save them from danger.

rest (rests, resting, rested)

1. *n.* If you have a *rest*, you stop what you have been doing for a while.
2. *n.* The *rest* means everything that is left.
3. *vb.* When you *rest*, you are still and relaxed.

restaurant (restaurants)

n. A *restaurant* is a place where people go and pay money to have a meal.

a   b   c   d   e   f   g   h   i   j   k   l   m

restless

   adj. People who are *restless*, cannot stay still for very long.

return (returns, returning, returned)

   1. *vb.* If you *return* something, you take it back.

   2. *vb.* If you *return* to a place, you go back to a place where you have been before.

reverse (reverses, reversing, reversed)

   1. *n.* The *reverse* of something is the opposite side of it.

   2. *vb.* When you *reverse*, you go backwards.

reward (rewards, rewarding, rewarded)

   1. *n.* A *reward* is a present that you get for doing something special.

   2. *vb.* If you *reward* someone, you give them something special to show you are pleased with them.

rhinoceros (rhinoceroses)

n. A *rhinoceros* is a big animal from Africa and Asia. It has a thick grey skin and two horns on its nose. *Rhinoceroses* eat grass and plants.

rhythm (rhythms)

   n. The *rhythm* in music is the beat.

rich (richer, richest)

   adj. If you are *rich*, you have a lot of money.

riddle (riddles)

   n. A *riddle* is a word puzzle with a funny answer.

ride (rides, riding, rode, ridden)

   1. *n.* A *ride* is a journey on a horse, on a bicycle, or in another vehicle.

   2. *vb.* If you *ride* a horse or a bicycle, you are on it while it is moving along.

rider (riders)

   n. A *rider* is someone who rides something like a horse or a bicycle. You can ride in cars, boats, trains and aeroplanes too.

right

   1. *adj. Right* is correct or true.

   2. *adj. Right* is the opposite of left.

ring (rings, ringing, rang)
1. *n.* A *ring* is a circle.
2. *n.* A show-jumping *ring* is a place where horses have a competition.
3. *vb.* If you *ring* a bell, you make it sound.

rip (rips, ripping, ripped)

vb. If you *rip* something, you tear it.

ripe (riper, ripest)
adj. If fruit is *ripe*, it is ready to be eaten.

rise (rises, rising, rose)
vb. When something *rises*, it goes up.

river (rivers)
n. A *river* is a large amount of fresh water that flows from high land to the sea.

road (roads)
n. A *road* is a long, hard piece of ground that takes traffic from one place to another.

roam (roams, roaming, roamed)
vb. If you *roam*, you wander about over a large area.

roar (roars, roaring, roared)
1. *n.* A *roar* is the loud, deep sound like the sound of a lion or of thunder.
2. *vb.* If you *roar*, you make a loud, rumbling noise.

roast (roasts, roasting, roasted)
vb. If you *roast* something, you cook it slowly in the oven.

robber (robbers)
n. A *robber* is a person who takes things that belong to other people without their permission.

robin (robins)
n. A *robin* is a bird with a red breast.

robot (robots)
n. A *robot* is a machine that is programmed to do particular jobs that people normally do, usually in factories.

rock (rocks)
n. A *rock* is a large piece of stone.

rocket (rockets)
1. *n.* A *rocket* is a firework joined to a stick.
2. *n.* A *rocket* is a tube filled with fast-burning fuel that is used to launch a spacecraft.

a b c d e f g h i j k l m

rocky (rockier, rockiest)

adj. A *rocky* place is covered with rocks.

rod (rods)

n. A *rod* is a straight stick or bar.

rode see **ride**

rodeo (rodeos)

n. A *rodeo* is a competition where cowboys try to stay on the back of a wild horse or bull.

roll (rolls, rolling, rolled)

1. *n.* A *roll* is a small, round or long piece of bread.
2. *vb.* If you *roll*, you turn over and over.

roller (rollers)

1. *n.* A *roller* is a large, heavy wheel.

2. *n.* A *roller* is the name of the machine that has a huge wheel on the front.

roof (roofs)

n. A *roof* is the top covering for a house or other building.

rookery (rookeries)

n. A *rookery* is a large number of rooks' nests high in the top of a group of trees.

room (rooms)

n. A *room* is one of the spaces inside a building that has its own walls, ceiling and floor. The kitchen, dining room and bedroom are all *rooms*.

roost (roosts, roosting, roosted)

vb. When birds *roost*, they settle down to sleep for the night.

root (roots)

n. The *root* of a plant is the part that grows underground.

rope (ropes)

n. *Rope* is made from very thick, strong pieces of string or wire which have been twisted together.

rose (roses)

n. A *rose* is a flower with a pleasant smell. Most *roses* have thorns on their stems.

rotten

1. *adj.* If something is *rotten*, it has gone bad.
2. *adj.* If you have a *rotten* time, you do not enjoy yourself.

rough (rougher, roughest)

1. *adj.* If something is *rough*, it is lumpy and bumpy.
2. *adj.* If the sea is *rough*, it has high waves.
3. *adj.* If you are *rough*, you are not gentle.

round (rounder, roundest)

adj. Something *round* is shaped like a circle or a ball.

roundabout (roundabouts)

1. *n.* A *roundabout* is a machine with seats on it. You can ride on *roundabouts* in parks and at fairgrounds.
2. *n.* A *roundabout* is a stone or grass circle in the middle of the road where several roads meet. You must drive around the roundabout until you reach the road where you want to turn off.

row (rows)

n. If things are in a *row*, they are in a line.

royal

adj. Royal means to do with the king and queen.

rub (rubs, rubbing, rubbed)

vb. If you *rub* something, you move your hand back and forwards on it.

rubbish

n. Rubbish is everything that you throw away.

rude (ruder, rudest)

adj. If you are *rude*, you are not well-behaved or polite.

rug (rugs)

n. A *rug* is a small carpet.

a b c d e f g h i j k l m

rule (rules)

n. A *rule* is a law that people should obey.

run (runs, running, ran)

vb. If you *run*, you use your legs to move very quickly.

rush (rushes, rushing, rushed)

1. *n.* A *rush* of air or water is the sound of it moving very quickly and suddenly.
2. *vb.* When you *rush,* you hurry.

rust (rusts, rusting, rusted)

1. *n. Rust* is a reddish-brown material that forms on metal when it has been wet.

2. *vb.* If metal *rusts,* it turns reddish-brown and begins to flake.

rustle (rustles, rustling, rustled)

1. *n.* If you hear a *rustle,* it sounds like the soft movement of dry leaves when the wind blows through them.
2. *vb.* If paper *rustles,* it makes a soft, crackly sound.
3. *vb.* If you hear something *rustling,* it might be an animal moving quietly in the bushes.

S s

sack (sacks)

n. A *sack* is a large bag made of cloth or plastic.

sad (sadder, saddest)

adj. If you are *sad*, you are unhappy about something.

saddle (saddles)

n. A *saddle* is a seat for an animal's back or a bicycle, so that you can ride on it comfortably.

safari (safaris)

n. A *safari* is a journey that a group of people make to watch or hunt wild animals.

safe (safer, safest)

adj. If you are *safe*, you are away from danger.

safely

adv. If you do something *safely*, you make sure you cannot be harmed while you are doing it.

safety

n. Safety is being safe.

said see **say**

sail (sails, sailing, sailed)

1. *n.* A *sail* is a large piece of material fixed to the mast of a ship or boat. When the sail fills with wind it makes the ship or boat move along.
2. *vb.* If a boat *sails* it moves across the water using the wind for power.

sailor (sailors)

n. A *sailor* is a person who works on a ship as a member of the crew.

saint (saints)

n. A *saint* is a holy person.

a b c d e f g h i j k l m

sale (sales)

n. A *sale* is a time when shops sell their goods cheaply.

salmon

n. *Salmon* are large fish that you can eat. They live in the sea but swim up rivers to lay their eggs.

salt

n. *Salt* is a white powder that you can add to food to give it flavour.

same

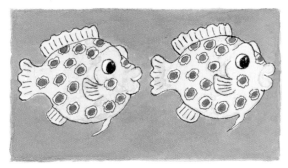

adj. If two things are the *same* they are exactly like each other.

sand

n. *Sand* is very tiny grains of rock that you find on beaches or in the desert.

sand castle (sand castles)

n. A *sand castle* is a model of a castle or a house made of sand.

sandwich (sandwiches)

n. A *sandwich* is made from two pieces of bread with a filling in between them.

sang see **sing**

sank see **sink**

sap

n. *Sap* is the liquid that carries food through plants and trees.

sardine (sardines)

n. A *sardine* is a small fish which you can eat. *Sardines* are often sold in tins.

sat see **sit**

satellite (satellites)

n. A *satellite* is something that moves in space around the earth or any other planet.

sauce (sauces)

n. A *sauce* is a thick, sweet or savoury liquid. It is usually served with food to make it taste more delicious.

saucepan (saucepans)

  n. A *saucepan* is a metal pot with a handle, which is used for cooking. It often has a lid.

saucer (saucers)

  n. A *saucer* is a small, round dish that you stand a cup on.

sausage (sausages)

  n. A *sausage* is made from very tiny pieces of meat mixed with other things like bread or herbs. You grill or fry a sausage before you eat it.

save (saves, saving, saved)

  1. *vb.* If you *save* someone, you get them out of danger.
  2. *vb.* If you *save* money, you collect it little by little.

saw see also **see**

say (says, saying, said)

  vb. When you *say* something, you speak.

scale (scales, scaling, scaled)

  1. *n. Scales* are the equipment used for weighing things.

  2. *n.* A *scale* is a set of musical notes.
  3. *n.* A *scale* is one of the small, flat pieces of skin that cover the bodies of fish or reptiles.
  4. *vb.* If you *scale* a mountain, you climb up its steep sides.

scare (scares, scaring, scared)

  1. *vb.* If you *scare* someone, you frighten them.
  2. *adj.* If you are *scared*, you are afraid.

scarecrow (scarecrows)

  n. A farmer uses a *scarecrow* to frighten birds away from the crops in the fields. A scarecrow usually looks like a person because it is dressed in old clothes.

scarf (scarves)

  n. A *scarf* is a long piece of material that you wear around your neck to keep you warm.

scary (scarier, scariest)

  adj. If something is *scary*, it is frightening.

scatter (scatters, scattering, scattered)

  vb. When you *scatter* things, you throw many small things over a wide area.

a b c d e f g h i j k l m

scent (scents)

1. *n.* Scent is perfume.
2. *n.* The *scent* of an animal is the smell it leaves behind it. Other animals can follow the scent trail if they are hunting it. The scent can also mark the animal's territory.

school (schools)

n. A *school* is a place where young people go to learn.

scientist (scientists)

n. A *scientist* is someone who finds out why things happen by doing tests and studying them carefully.

scissors

n. Scissors are tools for cutting. A pair of scissors has two blades that are joined together.

scoop (scoops, scooping, scooped)

1. *n.* A *scoop* is a deep spoon that can be used for serving ice-cream or mashed potato.
2. *vb.* If you *scoop* something up, you lift it with a scoop or with your hands shaped like a cup.

scramble (scrambles, scrambling, scrambled)

1. *vb.* If you *scramble,* you use your hands and feet to climb over, up or down something.
2. *vb.* If you *scramble* eggs, you beat eggs and milk together and cook them in a pan.

scrap (scraps, scrapping, scrapped)

1. *n.* A *scrap* is a small piece of something.
2. *n.* If you have a *scrap* with someone, you have a fight or a quarrel which is not too serious.
3. *vb.* If you *scrap* something, you throw it away.

scrap yard (scrap yards)

n. A *scrap yard* is a place where waste metal is collected and stored.

scratch (scratches, scratching, scratched)

1. *n.* A *scratch* is a thin cut or mark on your skin or on a piece of furniture where it has been damaged by something sharp.
2. *vb.* If something *scratches* you, it scrapes your skin and feels sharp.
3. *vb.* If you *scratch* an itch, you move your fingernails over your skin.

scream (screams, screaming, screamed)

1. *n.* A *scream* is a loud cry of pain or fear.

2. *vb.* If you *scream*, you cry out because you are frightened or hurt.

screech (screeches, screeching, screeched)
vb. If you *screech*, you make an unpleasant, loud, high-sounding noise.

scuttle (scuttles, scuttling, scuttled)
vb. If a person or an animal *scuttles*, it moves very quickly with little steps.

sea (seas)
n. A *sea* is a very large area of salt water.

seagull (seagulls)
n. A *seagull* is a large seabird.

seal (seals)
n. A *seal* is a large animal that eats fish and lives partly on land and partly in the sea.

sea-lion (sea-lions)
n. A *sea-lion* is a large seal.

search (searches, searching, searched)
vb. When you *search* for something, you look very hard for it.

seashore (seashores)

n. The *seashore* is the sandy, pebbly or rocky land next to the sea.

a b c d e f g h i j k l m

seaside (seasides)

n. The *seaside* is a place by the sea where people go for holidays.

seat (seats)

n. A *seat* is something to sit on.

sea urchin (sea urchins)

n. A *sea urchin* is a small, round sea creature with a spiky, hard shell.

seaweed (seaweeds)

n. Seaweed is a plant which grows in the sea.

second (seconds)

1. *n.* A *second* is a measure of time. There are 60 *seconds* in one minute.
2. *adj.* If you are *second* in a race, someone else is the winner but you are next.

secret (secrets)

n. A *secret* is something that only you and a few other people know about.

section (sections)

n. A *section* of something is part of it.

see (sees, seeing, saw, seen)

vb. If you *see* something, you use your eyes to look at it.

seed (seeds)

n. A *seed* is the small hard part of a plant that grows into a new plant when you put it into the ground.

see-saw (see-saws)

n. A *see-saw* is a plank of wood balanced on a fixed part in the middle. If you sit on one end and someone else sits on the other, you can take turns in going up and down.

seek (seeks, seeking, sought)

vb. If you *seek* someone or something, you look for them.

self (selves)

n. Your *self* is all your feelings and the way that you are.

selfish

adj. If you are *selfish*, you do not share anything with anyone else.

sell (sells, selling, sold)

vb. When you *sell* something, you let someone have it in return for money.

send (sends, sending, sent)

vb. If you *send* something, you make it go somewhere.

sense (senses)

n. Your *senses* are your power to see, feel, smell, taste and hear.

servant (servants)

n. A *servant* is a person who is paid to work in someone else's house.

serve (serves, serving, served)

1. *vb.* If you *serve* food, you give it to people, for example, in a cafe or restaurant.
2. *vb.* If someone *serves* a customer in a shop, they help them to find what they want to buy.

set (sets)

1. *n.* A *set* is a group of things which belong together.
2. *vb.* When something *sets*, it gets solid or hard.

sett (setts)

n. A *sett* is a badger's home.

several

adj. If you have *several* things, you have more than two but not many more.

sew (sews, sewing, sewed, sewn)

vb. If you *sew* something, you use a needle and thread to make stitches in it.

shade (shades, shading, shaded)

1. *n.* A *shade* is a cover for a light.
2. *vb.* If you *shade* something, you keep light away from it.
3. *vb.* If you *shade* a picture, you make parts of it darker with your pencil.

shadow (shadows)

n. A *shadow* is a patch of darkness that is made when there is something in the way of the light.

shaggy (shaggier, shaggiest)

adj. Something that is *shaggy* has long, untidy hair or fur.

a   b   c   d   e   f   g   h   i   j   k   l   m

shake (shakes, shaking, shook, shaken)
vb. If you *shake* something, you move it quickly up and down or from side to side.

shampoo (shampoos)

n. Shampoo is liquid soap that you use to wash your hair.

shape (shapes)
n. The *shape* of something is the way its outside edges look. The shape of a ball is round. A box is square.

share (shares, sharing, shared)
vb. When you *share* something, you give some of what you have to someone else.

shark (sharks)
n. A *shark* is a large sea fish with rows of sharp teeth.

sharp (sharper, sharpest)
adj. Something *sharp* has a thin edge or blade that is good for cutting things.

shawl (shawls)
n. A *shawl* is a large piece of cloth worn around the shoulders.

shed (sheds)
n. A *shed* is a small building that is used for storing things like garden tools.

sheep (sheep)
n. A *sheep* is a farm animal with a thick, woolly coat. *Sheep* are usually kept for their wool or their meat.

sheepdog (sheepdogs)
n. A *sheepdog* looks after the sheep with the farmer or the shepherd.

sheet (sheets)
n. A *sheet* is a large piece of cloth that you put on your bed.

sheikh (sheikhs)

n. A *sheikh* is an Arab leader.

shelf (shelves)

n. A *shelf* is a flat piece of wood, metal, or glass that is fixed to a wall or inside a cupboard. You can keep all kinds of things on a shelf.

shell (shells)

n. A *shell* is the thin, hard covering of an egg, a nut or some small animals like snails.

shellfish

n. Shellfish are all the sea creatures which have shells.

shelter (shelters)

n. A *shelter* is a place to hide in, or a place where you can keep dry when it rains.

shepherd (shepherds)

n. A *shepherd* is a person whose job is to look after sheep.

sheriff (sheriffs)

n. A *sheriff* is a person in America who is chosen to make sure that people obey the law.

shine (shines, shining, shone)

vb. When something *shines*, it gives out bright light.

shiny (shinier, shiniest)

adj. Something that is *shiny*, looks very bright.

ship (ships)

n. A *ship* is a large boat that sails on the sea.

shirt (shirts)

n. A *shirt* is a piece of clothing for the top half of the body.

shiver (shivers, shivering, shivered)

vb. If you *shiver*, you tremble because you are cold or frightened.

a b c d e f g h i j k l m

shock (shocks, shocking, shocked)
1. *n.* A *shock* is a surprise that is very unpleasant.
2. *vb.* If you *shock* someone, you do something that they do not expect.

shod see **shoe**

shoe (shoes, shoeing, shod)
1. *n.* *Shoes* are things that you wear on your feet to keep them warm and dry. Some shoes have shoelaces to do them up.
2. *vb.* If someone *shoes* a horse, they fix a new U-shaped piece of iron to the horse's hoof.

shook see **shake**

shoot (shoots, shooting, shot)
vb. If you *shoot*, you use a gun or a bow and arrow to fire at a target.

shop (shops, shopping, shopped)

1. *n.* A *shop* is a place where you can buy things.
2. *vb.* If you *shop* in a particular place, that is where you go to buy things.

shore (shores)
n. The *shore* is the dry land at the edge of a lake or a sea.

short (shorter, shortest)
1. *adj.* If something takes a *short* time, it happens quickly.
2. *adj.* If something is a *short* distance away, it is not far from where you are.
3. *adj.* If someone is *short*, they are not tall.

shotgun (shotguns)
n. A *shotgun* is a gun that fires many tiny lead balls. It is used for hunting wild birds and animals.

shoulder (shoulders)
n. Your *shoulder* is the place where your arm joins your body, near your neck.

shout (shouts, shouting, shouted)
1. *n.* A *shout* is a short, loud cry.
2. *vb.* If you *shout*, you call out very loudly.

shovel (shovels)

n. A *shovel* is a kind of curved spade for digging and lifting things such as coal and earth.

show (shows, showing, showed)

1. *n.* A *show* is an arrangement of things for people to look at.
2. *n.* A *show* is the performance of a play, music or dancing.
3. *vb.* If you *show* someone something, you let them look at it.

shower (showers, showering, showered)

1. *n.* A *shower* is a short, light fall of rain.
2. *n.* A *shower* is usually in a bathroom. You stand under a spray of water so that you can wash.
3. *vb.* When you *shower*, you wash yourself in a shower.

shrimp (shrimps)

n. A *shrimp* is a small shellfish.

shrine (shrines)

n. A *shrine* is a holy place where people go to worship.

shunt (shunts, shunting, shunted)

vb. When a train *shunts*, it pushes or pulls trucks or carriages from one track to another.

shut (shuts, shutting, shut)

1. *vb.* If you *shut* something like a door, you close it.
2. *adj.* Something that is *shut* is not open.
3. *adj.* If a shop is *shut*, you cannot go in to buy things.

shy (shyer, shyest)

adj. A *shy* person is afraid to meet people that they do not know.

sick (sicker, sickest)

adj. If you are *sick*, you are not well.

side (sides)

n. The *side* of something is the part to the left or right of the front and the back.

sieve (sieves)

n. A *sieve* is a bowl-shaped piece of wire netting in a frame that you use to sort large pieces from small pieces.

sift (sifts, sifting, sifted)

vb. When you *sift* something like flour, you use a sieve to make sure that there are no lumps in it.

a b c d e f g h i j k l m

sigh (sighs, sighing, sighed)
vb. If you *sigh,* you breathe out slowly and heavily so that other people can hear you.

sight (sights)
n. A *sight* is something that you can see.

sign (signs)

n. A *sign* is a piece of wood or metal with words or pictures on it.

signal (signals, signalling, signalled)

1. *n.* A *signal* is a sound or movement that tells people something without words.
2. *vb.* If you *signal* to someone, you send them a message without using words.

silence
n. *Silence* is no sound at all.

silk (silks)

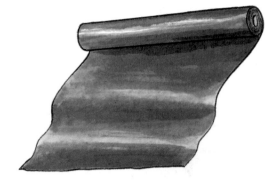

n. *Silk* is very fine, soft cloth made from thread spun by silkworms.

silly (sillier, silliest)
adj. If you are *silly,* you behave in a foolish or babyish way.

silver
n. *Silver* is a precious metal that is made into jewellery and ornaments.

simply
adv. Something that can be done or understood *simply,* is not difficult.

sing (sings, singing, sang, sung)
vb. When you *sing,* you make music with your voice.

single
adj. *Single* is only one of something.

sink (sinks, sinking, sank, sunk)
vb. If something *sinks,* it goes to the bottom of the water.

sir

You use the word *'sir'* when you are speaking politely to a man and not using his name.

sister (sisters)

n. Your *sister* is a girl who has the same parents as you.

sit (sits, sitting, sat)

vb. When you *sit,* you rest your weight on your bottom.

site (sites)

n. A building *site* is a place where building is going on.

size (sizes)

n. The *size* of something is how big or small it is.

skate (skates, skating, skated)

1. *n.* A *skate* is a boot that you wear to ice-skate or to roller-skate. Ice-skates have a blade fixed underneath and roller-skates have wheels.

2. *vb.* When you *skate,* you wear special boots so that you can travel smoothly over the ground or ice.

skateboard (skateboards)

n. A *skateboard* is a small board on wheels that you can stand on while it moves along.

skid (skids, skidding, skidded)

vb. If a vehicle *skids,* it slides sideways while it is moving because the road is slippery.

skill (skills)

n. Skill is being able to do something well. If you have musical *skills,* you are good at music.

skin (skins)

n. Skin covers the whole body of humans and other animals.

skip (skips, skipping, skipped)

vb. When you *skip,* you hop on one leg then the other, as if you are dancing.

skirt (skirts)

n. A *skirt* is a piece of clothing for girls and women to wear. *Skirts* hang from the waist.

a b c d e f g h i j k l m

skunk (skunks)

n. A *skunk* is a black and white animal that lives in North America. It lets out a bad smell when it is frightened.

sky (skies)

n. The *sky* is the space above the earth. The sun, moon and stars are in the sky.

slam (slams, slamming, slammed)

vb. If you *slam* something, you bang it hard.

sled (sleds)

n. A *sled* is the same as a sledge. It is an American word.

sledge (sledges)

n. A *sledge* is used for travelling over snow. It has strips of metal or wood underneath, so it will slide.

sleep (sleeps, sleeping, slept)

vb. When you *sleep*, you rest with your eyes shut and you do not know what is happening around you.

sleepy (sleepier, sleepiest)

adj. If you are *sleepy*, you are tired and ready to go to sleep.

sleeve (sleeves)

n. A *sleeve* is the part of a coat, shirt or dress that covers the arm.

slept see **sleep**

slice (slices, slicing, sliced)

vb. If you *slice* something, you take off a small, thin piece with a knife.

slide (slides, sliding, slid)

1. *n.* A *slide* is a long, slippery piece of metal that children slide down in a playground.
2. *vb.* If you *slide* on something, you move smoothly over it.

slime

1. *n. Slime* is a clear, sticky liquid that is left in a trail after slugs and snails.
2. *n. Slime* is a thick, green layer on top of water that has been still for a long time.

slimy (slimier, slimiest)

adj. If something is *slimy*, it is covered with a sticky liquid.

slip (slips, slipping, slipped)

vb. If you *slip*, you slide and sometimes fall down.

slipper (slippers)

n. A *slipper* is one of a pair of soft shoes that you wear in the house.

slither (slithers, slithering, slithered)

1. *vb.* If you *slither*, you slide and slip.
2. *vb.* If a snake *slithers*, it moves in a twisting way.

slow (slower, slowest)

adj. Things that are *slow*, do not move quickly.

slowly

adv. When you move *slowly*, you take a lot of time to move.

slug (slugs)

n. A *slug* is a small creature like a snail, but without a shell.

smack (smacks, smacking, smacked)

vb. If you *smack* someone, you hit them with the palm of your hand.

small (smaller, smallest)

adj. Someone or something that is *small* is little.

smart (smarter, smartest)

1. *adj.* If you are *smart* in the way you dress, you are neat and tidy.

2. *adj.* If you are *smart*, you are quick and clever.

smash (smashes, smashing, smashed)

vb. If you *smash* into something, you crash into it and break it.

smell (smells, smelling, smelled or smelt)

1. *vb.* If you *smell* something, you use your nose to find out about it.
2. *vb.* If something *smells*, you notice it with your nose.

smelly (smellier, smelliest)

adj. If something is *smelly*, it has a nasty smell.

a b c d e f g h i j k l m

smile (smiles, smiling, smiled)
1. *n.* A *smile* is a happy look on your face.
2. *vb.* When you *smile*, you make a wide shape with your lips to show you are happy.

smoke (smokes, smoking, smoked)

1. *n.* *Smoke* is a mixture of gas and soot that goes up into the air when something burns.
2. *vb.* When a person *smokes*, they suck in tobacco smoke through their mouths and breathe it out again.

smooth (smoother, smoothest)
adj. If something is *smooth*, it has no bumps or lumps in it.

snack (snacks)
n. A *snack* is a small, quick meal.

snail (snails)
n. A *snail* is a small creature that lives inside a shell. *Snails* move very slowly.

snake (snakes)
n. A *snake* is a long, thin reptile without legs. Some *snakes* are poisonous.

snap (snaps, snapping, snapped)
1. *vb.* If a dog *snaps*, it shuts its mouth suddenly as if it is biting.
2. *vb.* If you *snap* something, you break it suddenly.

snarl (snarls, snarling, snarled)
vb. If an animal *snarls*, it makes an angry, growling noise.

sniff (sniffs, sniffing, sniffed)
vb. If you *sniff*, you breathe in through your nose very noisily.

snore (snores, snoring, snored)

vb. When you *snore*, you breathe noisily when you are asleep.

snort (snorts, snorting, snorted)
vb. When you *snort*, you make a short, loud noise like a pig by making air go in through your nose very suddenly.

snow (snows, snowing, snowed)

1. *n. Snow* is small, thin, white flakes of frozen water that fall from the sky when the weather is very cold.
2. *vb.* When it *snows*, small white flakes fall from the sky.

soak (soaks, soaking, soaked)

vb. If you *soak* something, you make it very wet.

soap (soaps)

n. Soap is made from oil or fats. You use it to wash things. Sweet smells and colour are often added to make soap more pleasant to use.

sock (socks)

n. A *sock* is a piece of clothing for your foot. *Socks* come in pairs.

soft (softer, softest)

adj. If something is *soft*, it is not hard.

softly

adv. If you do something *softly*, you do it quietly and gently.

soil (soils)

n. Soil is earth that plants grow in.

sold see **sell**

soldier (soldiers)

n. A *soldier* is a person who works in an army.

solemn

adj. If you are *solemn*, you are serious.

solid (solids)

adj. Something *solid* is hard.

some

Some is a few. You say *someone*, if you mean a person, but not one person in particular. You say *something* if you mean a thing, but not one thing in particular. *Sometimes* is not always. *Somewhere* is a place, but not one particular place.

son (sons)

n. A *son* is a boy or man who is someone's child.

a b c d e f g h i j k l m

song (songs)

n. A *song* is a piece of music with words.

soon (sooner, soonest)

adv. If something happens *soon*, it happens in the near future.

sorry (sorrier, sorriest)

1. *adj.* If you feel *sorry* for someone, you feel sad because they are sad.
2. *'Sorry'* is what you say when you have done something wrong and you want to make up for it.

sort (sorts, sorting, sorted)

1. *n.* The *sort* of something is the kind or type it is. Chocolate drops and fruit gums are different *sorts* of sweets.

2. *vb.* If you *sort* things, you put them in groups that are alike in some way.

sound (sounds)

n. A *sound* is something that you can hear.

soup (soups)

n. *Soup* is a liquid food made of meat or vegetables.

source (sources)

n. The *source* of something is the place it came from.

south

n. *South* is one of the points of the compass.

southern

adj. Southern means in the south.

sow (sows) *rhymes with cow*

n. A *sow* is a female pig.

sow (sows, sowing, sowed) *rhymes with grow*

vb. If you *sow* a seed, you put it in the ground so that it will grow.

space (spaces)

1. *n. Space* is all the places beyond the earth. Spacemen explore space in spaceships.
2. *n.* A *space* is a place with nothing in it.

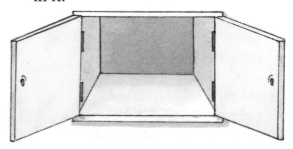

spaceship (spaceships)

n. A *spaceship* is a machine that takes people and things through space.

spatula (spatulas)

n. A *spatula* is like a broad, blunt knife. Artists and cooks use *spatulas* for spreading and mixing.

speak (speaks, speaking, spoke, spoken)

vb. When you *speak*, you open your mouth and say something.

spear (spears)

n. A *spear* is a weapon with a sharp point on the end of a long pole.

special

adj. *Special* things are usually better or more important than anything else.

specially

adv. If you do something *specially*, you do it for a particular reason.

speckled

adj. *Speckled* things are covered with small, coloured marks or spots.

speed (speeds)

n. The *speed* of something is how fast or how slowly it goes.

speedy (speedier, speediest)

adj. Something *speedy* is quick.

spell (spells, spelling, spelled or spelt)

1. *n.* A *spell* is a magic charm to make things happen.
2. *vb.* When you *spell* a word, you put the letters in the right order.

spend (spends, spending, spent)

vb. When you *spend* money, you use it to buy something that you want.

spice (spices)

n. *Spice* is the part of a plant that can be used whole, or ground up into powder and used to flavour food.

spider (spiders)

n. A *spider* is a small creature with eight legs. Most *spiders* make webs to catch insects for food.

a b c d e f g h i j k l m

spill (spills, spilling, spilled or spilt)
vb. If you *spill* something like milk, you accidentally let it fall out of a container.

spin (spins, spinning, spun)
1. *vb.* When you *spin*, you make thread by twisting long, thin pieces of cotton or wool together very quickly.
2. *vb.* When a spider or a caterpillar *spins*, it makes a web or a cocoon.
3. *vb.* If you *spin* something, you make it turn very quickly on a point.

spine (spines)
1. *n.* Your *spine* is your backbone.
2. *n.* The *spine* of a book is the narrow panel between the front and back covers where you can see the title and author.
3. *n.* A *spine* is one of the sharp, pointed hairs on the back of a hedgehog or on a sea urchin.

spiny (spinier, spiniest)

adj. Something *spiny* is covered with prickles.

spiral
adj. Something *spiral* winds round and round like a spring or the thread of a screw.

spire (spires)
n. A *spire* is the tall, pointed part on top of a church tower.

spirited
adj. If you are *spirited*, you are brave and lively.

splash (splashes, splashing, splashed)

vb. If you *splash*, you make drops of liquid fly up in the air with a loud noise.

splendid
adj. Something *splendid* is very good or very grand.

n o p q r **s** t u v w x y z

split (splits, splitting, split)
1. *vb.* If something *splits*, it cracks or tears.
2. *vb.* If you do the *splits*, you sit on the floor with one leg straight out in front of you and the other straight out behind you.

splutter (splutters, spluttering, spluttered)
vb. If you *splutter*, you make a lot of spitting sounds.

spoke see **speak**

spoken see **speak**

sponge (sponges)
1. *n.* A *sponge* is a light cake.

2. *n.* A *sponge* is soft and light and is full of tiny holes and can hold a lot of water. Some *sponges* are natural, from the sea, and some are man-made.

spoon (spoons)
n. A *spoon* is a tool with a long handle and a shallow bowl at the end that you use for eating.

sport (sports)
n. Sports are games like football, netball or tennis.

spot (spots, spotting, spotted)
1. *n.* A *spot* is a small mark on something.
2. *n.* A *spot* is a particular place like a quiet spot in the garden.
3. *vb.* If you *spot* someone or something, you notice them.

sprang see **spring**

spray (sprays, spraying, sprayed)
vb. If you *spray* water, you make it send out a lot of tiny drops of liquid over a large area.

spread (spreads, spreading, spread)
1. *vb.* If you *spread* something, you make it cover a large surface.
2. *vb.* If you *spread* something, you put a thin layer of it on to something.

spring (springs, springing, sprang)

1. *n. Spring* is a season.
2. *n.* A *spring* is a piece of coiled wire.
3. *vb.* If you *spring*, you jump into the air.

a   b   c   d   e   f   g   h   i   j   k   l   m

sprinkle (sprinkles, sprinkling, sprinkled)

vb. If you *sprinkle* something, you spread it around in small drops.

sprinter (sprinters)

n. A *sprinter* is someone who runs very fast over a short distance.

squash (squashes, squashing, squashed)

vb. If you *squash* something, you press it hard so that it loses its shape.

squawk (squawks, squawking, squawked)

vb. If a bird *squawks*, it makes a sudden, loud sound.

squeak (squeaks, squeaking, squeaked)

vb. If a person, an animal or a thing *squeaks*, it makes a tiny, high sound.

squeeze (squeezes, squeezing, squeezed)

vb. If you *squeeze* something, you press it between your hands.

squirrel (squirrels)

n. A *squirrel* is a small furry animal with a long bushy tail. It eats things like nuts and seeds. A squirrel's nest is called a drey.

squirt (squirts, squirting, squirted)

vb. If something *squirts*, it comes out of a small opening very quickly.

stable (stables)

n. A *stable* is a building where horses are kept.

stag (stags)

n. A *stag* is a fully-grown male deer.

stage (stages)

> *n.* A *stage* is a raised platform in a hall or a theatre. It is used for entertainers to perform on, or for speakers at meetings to be heard.

stair (stairs)

> *n. Stairs* are steps that go from one level to another. They are usually inside a building.

staircase (staircases)

> *n.* A *staircase* is a set of stairs.

stalk (stalks, stalking, stalked)

> 1. *n.* The *stalk* of a plant is its thin stem.

> 2. *vb.* If an animal *stalks* its prey, it quietly follows it until it can catch it.

stall (stalls)

> 1. *n.* A *stall* is a kind of small shop or table where things can be sold.
> 2. *n.* A *stall* is part of a stable or cowshed for one animal.

stamp (stamps, stamping, stamped)

> 1. *n.* A *stamp* is a small piece of sticky paper, usually with a picture on it. People put *stamps* on envelopes to post them.
> 2. *vb.* If you *stamp*, you bang your foot on the ground very hard.

stand (stands, standing, stood)

> *vb.* When you *stand*, you are on your feet and your legs are straight.

star (stars, starring, starred)

> 1. *n. Stars* are the tiny specks of bright light that you see in the sky at night.
> 2. *vb.* If a person or an animal *stars* in a film or a play, they have the most important part in it.

stare (stares, staring, stared)

> *vb.* If you *stare*, you look at someone or something without looking away.

start (starts, starting, started)

> 1. *n.* The *start* of something is the beginning of it.
> 2. *vb.* When something *starts*, it begins.

station (stations)

> 1. *n.* A *station* is a building where trains or buses stop for passengers.
> 2. *n.* A *station* is a building which is the headquarters of the police or fire service.

stay (stays, staying, stayed)

vb. If you *stay* somewhere, you go on being in the same place.

steal (steals, stealing, stole)

vb. If someone *steals*, they take something that does not belong to them.

steam (steams, steaming, steamed)

1. *n.* *Steam* is the hot mist that rises up from boiling water.
2. *vb.* If something *steams*, hot mist rises up from it.

steed (steeds)

n. A *steed* is an old-fashioned word for something to ride. It could be a horse or a bicycle.

steep (steeper, steepest)

adj. If something like a hill is *steep*, it slopes sharply.

steeple (steeples)

n. A *steeple* is a tall, pointed tower on top of a church.

steeplechase (steeplechases)

n. A *steeplechase* is a long horse race with hurdles and water jumps.

stem (stems)

n. The *stem* of a plant is the long, thin part in the middle. Leaves, fruit and flowers grow on a stem.

stencil (stencils)

n. A *stencil* is a cut-out shape that you can copy by pressing paint into the shape, or by drawing round it.

step (steps, stepping, stepped)

1. *n.* A *step* is a flat place to put your foot when you are walking up or down a slope.
2. *vb.* If you *step*, you lift your foot and put it down in another place.

stick (sticks, sticking, stuck)

1. *n.* A *stick* is a long, thin piece of wood.
2. *vb.* If you *stick* two things, you use glue to fix them together.

3. *adj.* If you are *stuck* in a small place, you cannot move.

stiff (stiffer, stiffest)

adj. If something is *stiff,* it is quite hard and will not bend.

still (stiller, stillest)

adj. If you sit *still,* you do not move.

sting (stings, stinging, stung)

vb. If something *stings* you, it gives you a sharp little stab of pain.

stir (stirs, stirring, stirred)

vb. When you *stir* a liquid or a mixture, you move it around with a spoon.

stockade (stockades)

n. A *stockade* is a high wall made of pointed wooden posts. A stockade is usually built to keep people or animals safe inside.

stolen see **steal**

stomach (stomachs)

n. Your *stomach* is the part of your body that holds food when you have eaten it.

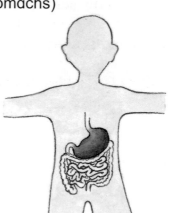

stone (stones)

n. A *stone* is a small piece of rock.

stood see **stand**

stool (stools)

n. A *stool* is a small seat with no back rest. It has short legs.

stop (stops, stopping, stopped)

vb. If you *stop* what you are doing, you do not do it anymore.

store (stores, storing, stored)

1. *n.* A *store* is a shop.
2. *vb.* If you *store* things, you put them away for later.

storm (storms)

n. A *storm* is very bad weather with strong winds and rain or snow. Sometimes there is thunder and lightning too.

a b c d e f g h i j k l m

story (stories)

n. A *story* can be written or spoken. A story tells you about something that has happened. It can be true or it can be made up.

straight (straighter, straightest)

adj. Something *straight* has no bends in it.

strand (strands)

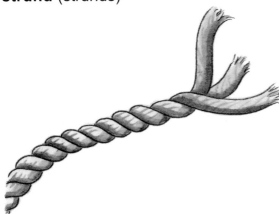

n. A *strand* is a thread that is twisted together with others to make a rope.

strange (stranger, strangest)

adj. Something that is *strange* is different, unusual or surprising.

stranger (strangers)

n. A *stranger* is someone you do not know.

straw (straws)

1. *n.* Straw is dry stalks of corn.
2. *n.* A *straw* is a thin tube that you use to drink through.

strawberry (strawberries)

n. A *strawberry* is a soft, red fruit.

street (streets)

n. A *street* is a road in a town with houses and a pavement.

strength

n. *Strength* is being able to lift or move heavy things.

stretch (stretches, stretching, stretched)

vb. When you *stretch*, you make yourself as big as you can. You often stretch when you are feeling tired.

strike (strikes, striking, struck)

1. *vb.* If you *strike* something, you hit it.
2. *vb.* When a clock or bell *strikes*, it makes a ringing sound.

n o p q r **s** t u v w x y z

string

   n. String is very thin rope.

stripe (stripes)

   n. A *stripe* is a coloured line across something.

stroke (strokes, stroking, stroked)

   vb. When you *stroke* an animal, you gently move your hand over it.

stroll (strolls, strolling, strolled)

   vb. If you *stroll,* you walk along in a slow and relaxed way.

strong (stronger, strongest)

   adj. People or animals that are *strong,* are fit and healthy and are able to carry heavy things.

strongman (strongmen)

   n. A *strongman* is a person who lifts very heavy weights as entertainment or in competitions.

struck see **strike**

struggle (struggles, struggling, struggled)

   1. *vb.* If you *struggle,* you try to free yourself from whatever is holding you, using your arms and legs.

   2. *vb.* If you *struggle* to do something, you try very hard to do it.

strut (struts, strutting, strutted)

   vb. If you *strut,* you walk in a stiff way, as if you are rather pleased with yourself.

stuck see **stick**

stud (studs)

   1. *n.* A *stud* is a metal fastening like a button.

   2. *n.* A *stud* is one of the knobs on the bottom of a sports boot which help you to grip.

study (studies, studying, studied)

   vb. When you *study,* you spend time learning about something.

stuff (stuffs, stuffing, stuffed)

   1. *n. Stuff* is a word that you use when you can't think of an exact name for something, or a collection of things.

   2. *vb.* If you *stuff* something, you fill it.

stumble (stumbles, stumbling, stumbled)

   vb. When you *stumble,* you fall over something.

stunt (stunts)

n. A *stunt* is a trick which is sometimes dangerous or daring.

stupid

adj. Someone who is *stupid*, does things that are not sensible.

style (styles)

1. *n.* Your *style* is the way you do something.
2. *n.* The *style* of something, like clothing, is the way it is made and how it looks.
3. *n.* If someone has *style*, they have a clever and attractive way of dressing and behaving.

subject (subjects)

n. A *subject* is what you learn about in a particular lesson.

suck (sucks, sucking, sucked)

vb. If you *suck* something, you draw in liquid or air from it with your mouth.

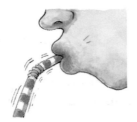

suckle (suckles, suckling, suckled)

vb. A young animal or baby *suckles*, when its mother feeds it with milk.

sudden

adj. If something is *sudden*, it happens quickly and without warning. It happens suddenly.

sugar

n. Sugar is powder or granules that you add to foods or drinks to sweeten them.

suit (suits)

n. A *suit* is a jacket with matching trousers or a skirt.

suitcase (suitcases)

n. A *suitcase* is a type of box with a lid and a handle that you use to carry your clothes and other things when you are going on holiday.

sulk (sulks, sulking, sulked)

vb. If you *sulk*, you are in a bad mood because you are annoyed and upset and do not want to talk to anyone.

sun (suns)

   n. The *sun* is the bright ball of fire in the sky that gives the earth heat and light.

sung see **sing**

sunny (sunnier, sunniest)

   adj. When it is *sunny,* the sun is shining.

sunrise (sunrises)

   n. Sunrise is the time in the early morning when the sun comes up.

sunshine

   n. Sunshine is the light and heat that the sun gives out.

super

   adj. Super means extra special.

supermarket (supermarkets)

   n. A *supermarket* is a large shop where you can buy all sorts of food and other goods.

supper (suppers)

   n. Supper is an early evening meal or a snack that you have before you go to bed.

supply (supplies, supplying, supplied)

   1. *n.* If you have a *supply* of something, you have enough to use.

   2. *vb.* If you *supply* something, you give it to someone who wants it.

suppose (supposes, supposing, supposed)

   vb. If you *suppose* something, you think it might be true although it might not be.

sure (surer, surest)

   adj. If you are *sure* about something, you are certain that it must be so.

surface (surfaces)

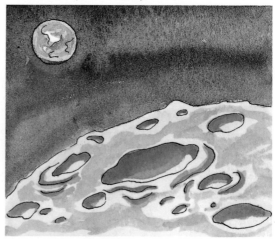

   n. The *surface* of something is the outside or top part of it.

a b c d e f g h i j k l m

surprise (surprises)

n. A *surprise* is something that happens when you are not expecting it.

surround (surrounds, surrounding, surrounded)

vb. If people, animals or things *surround* you, they are all around you.

surveyor (surveyors)

n. A *surveyor* is a person whose job is to look at a piece of land or a house very carefully before someone else buys it.

swallow (swallows, swallowing, swallowed)

1. *n.* A *swallow* is a bird with long wings and a tail with two points. Its body is dark blue.
2. *vb.* If you *swallow*, you make food or drink go down your throat.

swam see **swim**

swan (swans)

n. A *swan* is a large bird that lives on rivers and lakes. *Swans* are usually white with very long necks. Their young are called cygnets.

swarm (swarms, swarming, swarmed)

1. *n.* A *swarm* is a large number of bees together.
2. *vb.* If people, animals or insects *swarm*, they move together in a crowd.

sweep (sweeps, sweeping, swept)

1. *n.* A *sweep* is a person who cleans chimneys as a job.
2. *vb.* If you *sweep*, you clean things with a brush.

sweet (sweets; sweeter, sweetest)

1. *n.* A *sweet* is a small piece of sugary food like chocolate.
2. *adj.* *Sweet* food has sugar in it.

swiftly

adv. If you do something *swiftly*, you do it quickly.

swim (swims, swimming, swam, swum)

vb. If you *swim*, you use your arms and legs to move yourself through water without touching the bottom.

swimmer (swimmers)

n. Swimmers are people who can swim.

swing (swings)

1. *n.* A *swing* is a seat which hangs from posts or from a tree, for people to play on.

2. *vb.* When you *swing,* you make a hanging seat move backwards and forwards while you are sitting on it.
3. *vb.* If a monkey *swings* from tree to tree, it uses its arms to hold on to branches as it moves along.

swish (swishes, swishing, swished)

vb. If something *swishes*, it makes a soft hissing or rustling sound as it moves.

switch (switches, switching, switched)

1. *n.* A *switch* is a knob or button that you move to turn power on or off.
2. *vb.* If you *switch* to something different, you change to it.

swoop (swoops, swooping, swooped)

vb. When a bird *swoops*, it suddenly flies downwards through the air.

sword (swords)

n. A *sword* is a weapon with a long, sharp blade. It has a handle at one end.

symbol (symbols)

n. A *symbol* is a shape or pattern
that means something.

synagogue (synagogues)

n. A *synagogue* is a place where
Jews worship.

system (systems)

1. *n.* A *system* is a set of parts that
work together as one thing.
2. A *system* is a way of working or
doing something in a special order.

tabby (tabbies)

n. A *tabby* is a cat with striped fur.

table (tables)
> *n.* A *table* is a piece of furniture with a flat top for putting things on.

tablespoon (tablespoons)
> *n.* A *tablespoon* is a large spoon used for serving food or for measuring things.

tadpole (tadpoles)
> *n.* A *tadpole* is a baby frog. *Tadpoles* have long tails and round black heads.

tail (tails)
> *n.* A *tail* is the part of an animal, bird or fish that grows at the end of its body.

take (takes, taking, took, taken)
> 1. *vb.* If you *take* something, you get hold of it.
> 2. *vb.* If you *take* something somewhere, you move it from where it was to another place.

takeaway (takeaways)
> *n.* A *takeaway* is a cooked meal that you can buy in a shop or restaurant to eat somewhere else.

tale (tales)
> *n.* A *tale* is a story.

talk (talks, talking, talked)
> *vb.* When you *talk*, you speak to other people.

tall (taller, tallest)
> *adj.* Someone or something that is *tall* is very high.

talon (talons)
> *n.* *Talons* are the hooked claws of a bird of prey.

a b c d e f g h i j k l m

tambourine (tambourines)

n. A *tambourine* is a musical instrument that you shake or hit with your hands.

tame (tamer, tamest)

adj. If an animal is *tame*, it is not wild or dangerous.

tangle (tangles)

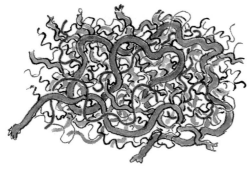

n. A *tangle* is a twisted muddle of things that is difficult to sort out.

tank (tanks)

1. *n.* A *tank* is a large container for liquid or gas.
2. *n.* A *tank* is a metal vehicle for soldiers.

tap (taps, tapping, tapped)

1. *n.* A *tap* is used to control the water that comes through a pipe.
2. *vb.* If you *tap* someone or something, you hit them lightly and quickly.

tarmac

n. *Tarmac* is a thick, sticky, black liquid that goes hard when it cools. It is used to make roads.

tartlet (tartlets)

n. A *tartlet* is a little, cooked pastry shape filled with something delicious.

taste (tastes, tasting, tasted)

1. *n.* *Taste* is one of the five senses that people and animals have. Your sense of taste makes it possible for you to recognise what you have in your mouth.
2. *vb.* When you *taste* something, you find out about it with your tongue.

tea (teas)

1. *n. Tea* is a drink made by pouring boiling water onto the dried leaves of the tea plant. Many people add milk and, often, sugar to their tea.

2. *n. Tea* is a small meal in the afternoon or evening.

teacher (teachers)

n. A *teacher* is a person whose job it is to help people to learn, usually in a school.

team (teams)

n. A *team* is a group of people who work together or play a sport together.

teapot (teapots)

n. A *teapot* is a container with a lid, a handle and a spout, used for making tea.

tear (tears)

rhymes with dear

n. Tears are drops of water that fall from your eyes when you are feeling unhappy.

tear (tears, tearing, tore, torn)

rhymes with bear

vb. If you *tear* something, you pull it apart and break it.

teaspoon (teaspoons)

n. A *teaspoon* is a small spoon that you use for stirring drinks and for measuring small amounts.

teatime (teatimes)

n. Teatime is the time in the afternoon when you have tea.

teat (teats)

n. Teats are the pointed parts of the bodies of female animals, which the young can suckle for milk.

teddy (teddies)

n. A *teddy* is a toy bear.

tee-shirt or **T-shirt** (tee-shirts or T-shirts)

n. A *tee-shirt* is a top made of soft, comfortable material.

a b c d e f g h i j k l m

teeth see **tooth**

telephone (telephones, telephoning, telephoned)
1. *n.* A *telephone* is a machine that you use to speak to people who are in another place and who are not with you.
2. *vb.* If you *telephone* someone, you dial their number and ask to speak to them on the telephone.

television (televisions)
n. A *television* is a machine that brings pictures and sound through the air by electricity. *TV* is short for television.

tell (tells, telling, told)
vb. If you *tell* someone something, you pass on a story or information by speaking or writing to them.

tempo (tempos)
n. The *tempo* of a piece of music is how fast you should play it.

tent (tents)

n. A *tent* is a shelter made of canvas. You use a tent when you go camping.

tentacle (tentacles)

n. Tentacles are the long, thin, snake-like parts of animals like the octopus.

terrace (terraces)

n. A *terrace* is a row of houses or cottages all joined together.

terrible
adj. If something is *terrible*, it is very, very bad.

terrific
adj. If something is *terrific*, you are very, very pleased by it.

territory (territories)
n. Territory is land that belongs to a particular group of people or a country.

test (tests, testing, tested)

1. *n.* A *test* is some questions to find out how much you know about something.
2. *vb.* If you *test* something, you try it out to see if it works.

thank (thanks, thanking, thanked)

vb. If you *thank* someone, you show that you are pleased about something they have done for you.

their (theirs)

If something is *theirs*, it belongs to them.

them see **they**

themselves

When you use the word '*themselves*', you mean the people and things you are talking about and no one else.

then

1. *adv.* *Then* means a time in the past or a time in the future.
2. *adv.* *Then* is another word for next.

these see **this**

they

They are the people, animals or things that you are talking about.

thick (thicker, thickest)

1. *adj.* If something is *thick*, it is not thin. It is wide and fat.

2. *adj.* If a liquid is *thick*, it is not runny.
3. *adj.* If you have *thick* hair, the strands grow closely and you have a lot of it.

thief (thieves)

n. A *thief* is a person who takes things that belong to someone else, without asking.

thin (thinner, thinnest)

adj. Something that is *thin* is narrow. It is not fat or thick.

thing (things)

n. A *thing* is anything that can be seen and touched. If you do not know what something is called you say it is a 'thing'.

think (thinks, thinking, thought)

vb. When you *think*, you have words and ideas in your mind.

thirsty (thirstier, thirstiest)

adj. If you are *thirsty*, you need a drink.

this (these)

When you say *this* one, you mean the one here.

thistle (thistles)

n. A *thistle* is a wild plant with prickly leaves and purple flowers.

thistledown

n. *Thistledown* is the white seed heads of the thistle.

thong (thongs)

n. A *thong* is a long strip of leather.

thorax (thoraxes)

n. Your *thorax* is the part of your body between your neck and your waist.

those see **that**

thought see **think**

thread (threads, threading, threaded)

1. n. A *thread* is a thin piece of something like cotton, wool or nylon.

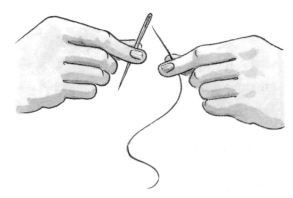

2. vb. When you *thread* a needle, you put cotton through the eye so that you can sew with it.

threw see **throw**

throat (throats)

n. Your *throat* is the top of the tube that takes the food from your mouth into your stomach.

through

adv. If you go *through* something, you go from one side to the other, or from one end to the other.

n o p q r s t u v w x y z

throw (throws, throwing, threw, thrown)

vb. When you *throw* something like a ball, you send it into the air with your hand.

thrush (thrushes)

n. A *thrush* is a garden bird. It has a cream breast with brown spots on it. The song of a thrush is very beautiful.

thump (thumps, thumping, thumped)

1. *n.* A *thump* is a loud noise made by something heavy hitting the ground.
2. *vb.* If you *thump* somebody, you hit them with your fist.

thunder (thunders, thundering, thundered)

1. *n. Thunder* is a loud noise in a storm. There is usually a loud rumble after lightning.
2. *vb.* If someone's voice *thunders*, it is very loud, deep and scary.

thunderbolt (thunderbolts)

n. A *thunderbolt* is a clap of thunder with a flash of lightning that strikes something like a tree.

tick (ticks, ticking, ticked)

1. *n.* A *tick* is a mark like a V with a long right side. It means that something is correct.
2. *vb.* If something *ticks*, it makes a sound like a clock.

tickle (tickles, tickling, tickled)

vb. If you *tickle* someone, you move your fingers quickly and lightly on their body to make them laugh.

tidal

adj. A *tidal* lake or river has a different water level as the sea goes in and out.

a b c d e f g h i j k l m

tide (tides)

n. The *tide* is the movement of the sea.

tidy

(tidies, tidying, tidied)

vb. If you *tidy*, you put things away in their proper place so that everything looks neat.

tie (ties, tying, tied)

1. vb. If you *tie* something, you fix it together with string or rope.
2. vb. If you *tie* someone up, you use ropes to stop them getting away.

tiger (tigers)

n. A *tiger* is a large, wild animal found in India and China. It has orange and black striped fur. A female tiger is called a *tigress*.

tight (tighter, tightest)

adj. *Tight* is not loose. Something that is tight fits very closely.

till (tills)

n. A *till* is a machine for keeping money safe in a shop.

timber (timbers)

n. *Timber* is wood that has been cut down.

time (times)

n. *Time* is what we measure in units of seconds, minutes, hours, days, weeks and so on.

tin (tins)

1. n. *Tin* is soft, silvery-white metal.
2. n. A *tin* is a container made from tin or aluminium.

tinkle (tinkles, tinkling, tinkled)

vb. If something *tinkles*, it sounds like tiny bells.

tinned

adj. *Tinned* food is kept from going bad by being packed and sealed in a tin.

tiny (tinier, tiniest)

adj. Something *tiny* is very, very small.

tip (tips, tipping, tipped)

1. *n.* A *tip* is a place where you can throw away rubbish.
2. *n.* If you give someone like a waiter or a hairdresser a *tip*, you give them a small amount of money because you are pleased with the way they have looked after you.
3. *n.* The *tip* is the end of something.
4. *vb.* If you *tip* something, you turn it over so that things inside fall out.

tipper (tippers)

n. A *tipper* is a lorry which can be raised up at the back to let the load it is carrying slide out onto the ground.

tired

adj. When you are *tired*, you want to rest or go to sleep.

tit (tits)

n. A *tit* is a small garden bird.

toad (toads)

n. A *toad* is an animal like a big frog. It has rough, dry skin and lives in damp places on land.

toast (toasts, toasting, toasted)

1. *n.* *Toast* is bread which is cooked until it is brown and crisp.
2. *vb.* When you *toast* bread, you cook it in a toaster or under a grill until it is brown and crisp.

toboggan (toboggans, tobogganing, tobogganed)

1. *n.* A *toboggan* is a kind of sledge for riding on snow.
2. *vb.* When you *toboggan*, you ride on a toboggan for fun.

today

adv. *Today* is the day that it is now.

toe (toes)

n. A *toe* is one of the five separate parts at the end of your foot.

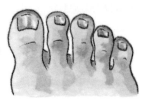

together

adv. If you do things *together*, you do them with other people.

told see **tell**

tomato (tomatoes)

n. A *tomato* is a small, red fruit that you can eat raw in salads, cooked as a vegetable or in sauces.

a b c d e f g h i j k l m

tomorrow

adv. Tomorrow is the day after today.

tongue (tongues)

n. Your *tongue* is the soft piece of flesh in your mouth that you can move. Your tongue helps you to taste, to eat and to speak.

tonight

adv. Tonight is this evening or night.

tonne (tonnes)

n. A *tonne* is a unit of weight. It is equal to 1,000 kilograms.

tooth (teeth)

n. A *tooth* is one of the hard, white objects that grow in your mouth. You use your *teeth* to bite and eat food.

toothache

n. Toothache is a pain in your tooth.

toothbrush (toothbrushes)

n. A *toothbrush* is a small brush with a long handle that you use to clean your teeth.

toothpaste (toothpastes)

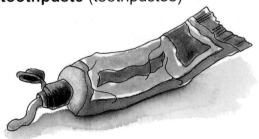

n. Toothpaste is a paste that you use to clean your teeth.

top (tops)

n. The *top* of something is the highest part of it.

torn see **tear**

tornado (tornadoes)

n. A *tornado* is a huge storm with very strong winds. The centre of the storm is a cloud shaped like a funnel.

tortoise (tortoises)

n. A *tortoise* is a small animal with a shell that covers its body. It moves very slowly.

tortoiseshell (tortoiseshells)

n. Tortoiseshell is the shell of a sea-turtle. It is yellow and brown and is sometimes polished to make ornaments and jewellery.

toss (tosses, tossing, tossed)

vb. If you *toss* something, you throw it lightly into the air.

touch (touches, touching, touched)

vb. If you *touch* something or someone, you feel them by putting your hand on them.

tough (tougher, toughest)

1. *adj.* If food is *tough,* it is hard to chew.
2. *adj.* Someone or something *tough,* is strong and difficult to break.

tousle (tousles, tousling, tousled)

vb. If you *tousle* someone's hair, you ruffle it with your fingers.

toward or **towards**

If you move *towards* something, you go nearer to it.

towel (towels)

n. A *towel* is a large cloth that you use to dry yourself after washing.

tower (towers)

n. A *tower* is a very tall, narrow building.

town (towns)

n. A *town* is a place with a lot of streets and buildings where people live and work.

toy (toys)

n. A *toy* is something you play with.

track (tracks, tracking, tracked)

1. *n.* A *track* is a special path where people and animals can practise running.
2. *n.* A *track* is a rough path through a wood or a farm.

3. *vb.* If a dog *tracks* a missing object or person, it uses its nose to find them.

a b c d e f g h i j k l m

tractor (tractors)

   n. A *tractor* is a farm machine that can pull heavy weights. It has very large wheels at the back.

traditional

   adj. Something that is *traditional* has been going on in the same way for many years.

traffic

   n. Traffic is many cars, lorries, motorbikes, buses, bicycles and other things that travel on the road.

trail (trails)

   1. *n.* A *trail* is a rough path.
   2. *n.* A *trail* is a scent that animals leave behind them.
   3. *n.* The *trail* of a snail is the silvery mark it leaves behind it when it slides along.

trailer (trailers)

   n. A *trailer* is a cart or a large container which is pulled by another vehicle.

train (trains, training, trained)

   1. *n.* A *train* has carriages which are joined together and is pulled by an engine. *Trains* travel along railway tracks.
   2. *vb.* If you *train* an animal, you teach it to do things.
   3. *vb.* If you *train* to do something like a sport, you practise so that you get better at it.

tram (trams)

   n. A *tram* is a type of bus that runs on rails and gets its power from overhead cables.

transporter (transporters)

   n. A *transporter* is a very large lorry that carries heavy loads from one place to another.

trap (traps)

   n. A *trap* is something for catching animals or insects.

travel (travels, travelling, travelled)

   vb. When you *travel,* you go from one place to another.

traveller (travellers)

n. A *traveller* is a person who travels around and doesn't stay in one place for long.

tray (trays)

n. A *tray* is a flat piece of wood or plastic which you use to carry things, usually food and drinks.

treacle

n. *Treacle* is a very thick, dark, sticky liquid. Treacle is used in making puddings and cakes.

treasure (treasures)

n. *Treasure* is gold, silver and precious jewels.

treat (treats, treating, treated)

1. *n.* A *treat* is a special event or something special to eat.
2. *vb.* If you *treat* someone, you give them something special.

tree (trees)

n. A *tree* is a large plant with a trunk made of wood. It has branches and leaves on it.

trek (treks, trekking, trekked)

1. *n.* A *trek* is a long and very tiring journey.
2. *vb.* If you go on a *trek,* you travel a long way over rough ground, on horse-back or on foot.

tremble (trembles, trembling, trembled)

vb. If you *tremble,* you shiver because you are afraid of what is going to happen.

tress (tresses)

n. A woman's *tresses* are her long hair. It is an old-fashioned word.

triangle (triangles)

n. A *triangle* is a flat shape with three sides and three corners.

trick (tricks)

n. A *trick* is a clever thing to do to entertain people.

a b c d e f g h i j k l m

trip
(trips, tripping, tripped)
1. *n.* A *trip* is a journey that you make to a place and back again.
2. *vb.* If you *trip*, you fall over something.

troll (trolls)
n. A *troll* is an imaginary, unpleasant creature that you read about in stories from Scandinavia. They are supposed to look like ugly humans and roam around at night. *Trolls* are said to turn to stone at daybreak.

trolley (trolleys)

n. A *trolley* is a wire basket on wheels that you use to collect all your shopping in a supermarket.

troop (troops, trooping, trooped)
1. *n.* *Troops* are all the men and women serving in an army.
2. *vb.* If a group of people *troop* somewhere, they all go along together.

trot (trots, trotting, trotted)
vb. When a horse or pony *trots*, it moves faster than a walk.

trouble (troubles)
n. *Trouble* is something that makes people upset or worries you.

trousers
n. *Trousers* are a piece of clothing that cover your legs and the lower part of your body.

trout (trouts)

n. *Trout* are large fish that are good to eat. They are found in rivers and streams.

trowel (trowels)
n. A *trowel* is a little spade for digging in the garden.

truck (trucks)
n. A *truck* is a type of lorry.

true (truer, truest)

adj. If something is *true*, it is real and not made-up.

trunk (trunks)

1. *n.* A *trunk* is a huge case or box for taking a lot of clothes or other things from one place to another safely.
2. *n.* A *trunk* is an elephant's nose.

trust (trusts, trusting, trusted)

vb. If you *trust* someone, you believe that they will not let you down or hurt you in any way.

truth (truths)

1. *n.* If you tell the *truth*, you do not tell lies.
2. *n.* The *truth* is something that actually happened.

try (tries, trying, tried)

vb. If you *try* to do something, you do your best to do it.

tube (tubes)

n. A *tube* is a hollow shape like a pipe.

tuck (tucks, tucking, tucked)

1. *vb.* If you *tuck* something in, you tidy the loose ends away.
2. *vb.* If you *tuck* someone in at bedtime, you make sure they are warm and comfortable with the bedclothes all around them.

tug (tugs, tugging, tugged)

vb. If you *tug* something, you pull it hard.

tug-of-war (tugs-of-war)

n. A *tug-of-war* is a competition between two teams who pull on a big rope to see which team is the strongest.

tumble (tumbles, tumbling, tumbling)

vb. If you *tumble*, you fall or roll over and over.

tummy (tummies)

n. Your *tummy* is your stomach.

tuna

n. Tuna are large fish that live in warm seas. Tuna fish can be eaten.

a b c d e f g h i j k l m

tunnel (tunnels)

n. A *tunnel* is a long hole or passage which is under the ground.

turn (turns, turning, turned)
1. *n.* When it is your *turn* to do something, it is your go.
2. *vb.* When you *turn,* you move to face a different way.

turnip (turnips)
n. A *turnip* is a round, white vegetable that grows underground.

turtle (turtles)
n. A *turtle* is a large sea creature with a thick shell.

TV see **television**

tusk (tusks)
n. A *tusk* is one of the long, pointed teeth of an elephant, walrus or wild boar.

twice
Twice means two times.

twig (twigs)
n. A *twig* is a tiny branch on a tree or a bush.

twist (twists, twisting, twisted)
vb. If you *twist* something, you turn one part of it to face a different direction.

type (types, typing, typed)
1. *n.* The *type* of something is the sort that it is.
2. *vb.* If you *type* something, you use a typewriter to write the words.

typewriter (typewriters)
n. A *typewriter* is a machine that has keys on it for each letter of the alphabet. When the typist presses the keys, the letters are printed on paper.

typhoon (typhoons)
n. A *typhoon* is a violent, windy storm.

ugly (uglier, ugliest)

adj. Someone who is *ugly* is not pleasant to look at.

unable

adj. If you are *unable* to do something, you cannot do it.

uncle (uncles)

n. An *uncle* is the brother of your father or mother.

under

Under means below.

underground

n. *Underground* means under the ground.

underneath

Underneath means that other things are on top.

unfurled

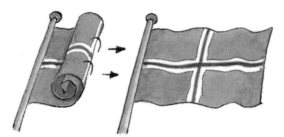

adj. When a flag or sail is *unfurled*, it is unrolled.

unhappy (unhappy, unhappiest)

adj. Someone who is *unhappy* is very sad.

unicorn (unicorns)

n. A *unicorn* is an imaginary animal like a white horse with one horn growing from its forehead.

a b c d e f g h i j k l m

uniform (uniforms)

n. A *uniform* is a special set of clothes that people wear to show the job that they do or the school that they go to.

unit (units)

n. A *unit* is one complete thing.

untie (unties, untying, untied)

vb. If you *untie* something, you undo it.

until

Until means up to the time when something else happens.

untwist (untwists, untwisting, untwisted)

vb. If you *untwist* something, you make it straight.

unusual

adj. Something *unusual* is rare or different.

upper

adj. *Upper* is the highest part of something.

upright

adj. If something is *upright*, it is the right way up.

upstairs

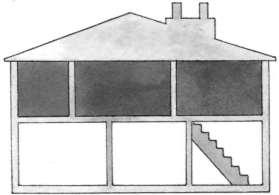

n. *Upstairs* is the top part of a house that you reach by climbing a staircase.

upwards

adj. If someone or something goes *upwards*, they move to a higher place.

urchin (urchins)

n. An *urchin* is the old-fashioned word for a poor homeless child.

use (uses, using, used)

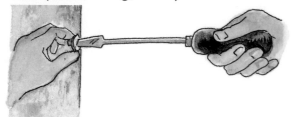

vb. If you *use* something like a tool, you do something with it to help you.

useful

adj. If something is *useful*, it can help you.

usual

adj. If something is *usual*, it is what normally happens.

usually

adv. If you *usually* do something, you often do it.

utensil (utensils)

n. *Utensils* are the tools that you use in the kitchen.

Vv

vacuum (vacuums)

1. *n.* A *vacuum* is a space which contains no air.
2. *vb.* If you *vacuum* something, you clean it using a vacuum cleaner.

valley (valleys)

n. A *valley* is a low stretch of land between hills. Often rivers flow through *valleys*.

vampire (vampires)

n. A *vampire* is a creature in scary stories. *Vampires* have sharp, pointed teeth called fangs.

van (vans)

n. A *van* is a small covered truck for carrying things from place to place.

vanilla

n. *Vanilla* is a flavouring for sweet food. It is made from the pods of the vanilla plant.

variegated

adj. *Variegated* leaves have different coloured markings on them.

vegetable (vegetables)

n. A *vegetable* is a plant which is eaten raw or cooked. Potatoes, cabbages and beans are *vegetables*.

vehicle (vehicles)

n. A *vehicle* is anything that takes people from one place to another. Cars, vans, buses, carts and lorries are all *vehicles*.

velvet

n. *Velvet* is a soft material that feels furry on one side.

Venus

n. *Venus* is one of the smaller planets but shines brightly in the morning and evening sky.

vermicelli

n. *Vermicelli* is very thin pasta, like spaghetti.

verse (verses)

n. A *verse* is one part of a song or a poem.

vessel (vessels)

1. *n.* A *vessel* is a ship or a boat.
2. *n.* A *vessel* is a container like a large jar or bowl for liquid. This is an old-fashioned word.
3. *n.* A *vessel* is a thin tube in your body, or in a plant, in which liquid can move.

vicar (vicars)

n. A *vicar* is a priest in the Church of England. He leads services in church, and helps people who live in his area.

victorious

adj. If you are *victorious*, you are successful in a battle.

village (villages)

n. A *village* is a small group of houses, usually in the country. There is often a church, a shop, a school and a pub in a village.

villager (villagers)

n. A *villager* is a person who lives in a village.

viper (vipers)

n. A *viper* is a poisonous snake.

visit (visits, visiting, visited)

vb. If you *visit* someone, you go to see them.

visitor (visitors)

n. Someone who visits is called a *visitor*.

vitamin (vitamins)

n. Vitamins are things that people need to eat to stay healthy. If you eat sensibly, you will have all the *vitamins* that you need.

vixen (vixens)

n. A *vixen* is a female fox.

voice (voices)

n. Your *voice* is the sound you make when you speak or sing.

volcano (volcanoes)

n. A *volcano* is a mountain with a crater at the top. Some *volcanoes* erupt and send hot ash and lava down their slopes.

vole (voles)

n. A *vole* is a small mouse-like animal that lives in hedges. It has short ears and a tail.

waddle (waddles, waddling, waddled)
vb. If you *waddle,* you take short steps and rock your body from side to side like a duck.

wag (wags, wagging, wagged)

vb. When a dog *wags* its tail, it moves it quickly from side to side because it is pleased to see you.

wagon (wagons)
n. A *wagon* is a strong cart with four wheels that a farmer uses to move heavy loads. In the past it was often pulled by horses or oxen.

wail (wails, wailing, wailed)
vb. If you *wail,* you let out a long, high cry.

wait (waits, waiting, waited)
vb. If you *wait,* you spend some time before anything happens or before you can do anything.

wake (wakes, waking, woke, woken)
1. *vb.* When you *wake,* you stop being asleep.
2. '*Wake up!*' is what you hear if you have slept in and you are late for school.

walk (walks, walking, walked)
1. *n.* A *walk* is a journey on foot.

2. *vb.* When you *walk,* you put one foot in front of the other to move along.

wall (walls)
1. *n.* A *wall* is used to divide two pieces of land. It is usually made of bricks or stone.
2. *n.* A *wall* is one side of a room.

a b c d e f g h i j k l m

walrus (walruses)

n. A *walrus* is an animal that lives in the sea. It looks like a big seal. It has long tusks and a hairy face. *Walruses* usually come from the Arctic.

waltzer (waltzers)

n. A *waltzer* is a ride at a fairground.

wand (wands)

n. A magician uses a *wand* to make magic spells work.

wander (wanders, wandering, wandered)

vb. If you *wander,* you walk about without trying to go anywhere in particular.

wanderer (wanderers)

n. A *wanderer* is a person who goes from place to place without deciding where to go before setting off.

war (wars)

n. A *war* is a fight between countries that may go on for a long time.

ward (wards)

n. A *ward* is a large room in a hospital with lots of beds for patients who are ill and where nurses and doctors can look after them.

warden (wardens)

n. A *warden* looks after something like a block of flats or a road crossing.

wardrobe (wardrobes)

n. A *wardrobe* is a cupboard where you can keep your clothes.

warm (warmer, warmest)

adj. Something *warm* is almost hot.

warn (warns, warning, warned)
vb. If you *warn* someone, you tell them that they might be in danger.

warren (warrens)
n. A *warren* is lots of rabbits' burrows together in the same place.

wash (washes, washing, washed)
1. *vb.* When you *wash*, you use water and soap to clean yourself.
2. *vb.* If you *wash* clothes, you clean them with soap and water and hang them to dry on a washing line.

wasp (wasps)

n. A *wasp* is a yellow and black striped insect with wings. *Wasps* can give you a nasty sting.

waste (wastes, wasting, wasted)
1. *n.* *Waste* is rubbish or things that people do not want or need.
2. *vb.* If you *waste* something, you leave it or throw it away because you have too much.

watch (watches, watching, watched)

1. *n.* A *watch* is a small clock that you wear on your wrist.
2. *vb.* If you *watch* something, you look at it for a long time.
3. When you call '*Watch out!*', you warn someone of danger.

water (waters, watering, watered)
1. *n.* *Water* is a clear liquid that falls from the sky as rain and flows in rivers to the sea.
2. *vb.* If you *water* a plant, you pour water on it to help it grow.

waterproof
adj. *Waterproof* things keep out the wet.

wave (waves, waving, waved)
1. *n.* A *wave* is a line of water that moves in the sea.
2. *vb.* If you *wave*, you move your hand backwards and forwards to say goodbye or hello to someone.

wax (waxes)
n. *Wax* is made of oil which melts when it is heated and becomes solid when it is cold. Wax is used to make candles and polish.

a b c d e f g h i j k l m

way (ways)

1. *n.* The *way* to somewhere is the direction you go to get there.
2. *n.* The *way* you do something is how you do it.

weak (weaker, weakest)
adj. If something is *weak*, it has no strength.

wealthy (wealthier, wealthiest)

adj. People who are *wealthy* have a great deal of money.

wear (wears, wearing, wore)
vb. When you *wear* clothes, you have them on your body.

weather
n. *Weather* is what it is like outside each day. Rain, snow, sun, fog and wind are all part of the weather.

weave (weaves, weaving, wove, woven)
vb. If you *weave* cloth you make it by crossing the threads over and under each other on a loom.

web (webs)
n. A *web* is a thin net that spiders make to catch their prey.

wedding (weddings)

n. A *wedding* is when two people get married.

weed (weeds, weeding, weeded)

1. *n.* A *weed* is a plant that grows where you do not want it to grow.
2. *vb.* If you *weed* a garden, you take away all the plants you do not want.

week (weeks)
n. A *week* is seven days.

weigh (weighs, weighing, weighed)
vb. When you *weigh* something or someone, you use scales to find out how heavy they are.

weight (weights)

n. *Weight* is how heavy something is.

welcome (welcomes, welcoming, welcomed)

vb. When you *welcome* someone, you greet them in a friendly way.

well (wells)

1. n. A *well* is a deep hole in the ground which has been dug to reach or hold water.
2. adv. If something grows *well*, it gets better and better.
3. adv. If you sleep *well*, you have a good sleep.

west

n. *West* is one of the points of the compass.

wet (wetter, wettest)

adj. If something is *wet*, it is covered with liquid.

whale (whales)

n. A *whale* is the largest sea animal there is. *Whales* are mammals.

wheel (wheels, wheeling, wheeled)

1. n. A *wheel* is a round object that you see on cars, trains and bicycles. The wheel goes round and the vehicle moves.

2. vb. If you *wheel* something, you move it on wheels.

wheelchair (wheelchairs)

n. A *wheelchair* is a seat on wheels that old or ill people use to help them move around.

whelk (whelks)

n. A *whelk* is a shellfish like a snail, that can be eaten.

whimper (whimpers, whimpering, whimpered)

vb. When a person or animal *whimpers*, they make a low, moaning noise because they are afraid or in pain.

a b c d e f g h i j k l m

whip (whips, whipping, whipped)

1. *n.* A *whip* is a thin cane or a leather strap that can be used to beat a person or an animal.
2. *vb.* If you *whip* a person or an animal, you beat them with a whip.
3. *vb.* If you *whip* cream, you beat it until it thickens.

whirlwind (whirlwinds)

n. A *whirlwind* is a wind that pulls everything towards its centre.

whisk (whisks, whisking, whisked)
vb. If you *whisk* food, you stir air into it very quickly.

whisper (whispers, whispering, whispered)
vb. When you *whisper,* you speak very quietly so only a few people can hear.

whistle (whistles, whistling, whistled)

vb. You *whistle* when you blow air through a small gap between your lips. *Whistling* is a very high, sharp sound.

white (whiter, whitest)
adj. Something that is *white* is the colour of snow.

whole
n. The *whole* of something is all of it.

wholemeal
adj. Wholemeal bread is made from the grains and the husks of the wheat. Nothing is taken out.

wicked
adj. If a person is *wicked,* they are very bad and unpleasant.

wide (wider, widest)
adj. Something *wide* measures a long way from side to side.

wife (wives)
n. A *wife* is a married woman.

wiggle (wiggles, wiggling, wiggled)
vb. When you *wiggle,* you move from side to side and up and down.

wild (wilder, wildest)
adj. Wild animals live in the fields, jungles and forests. They are not tame and are not used to living with people.

willow (willows)

n. A *willow* is a type of tree that grows near water. It has long, narrow leaves and its branches often droop downwards.

win (wins, winning, won)
vb. If you *win* a race or a competition, you come first.

wind (winds)
n. The *wind* is the moving of air across the earth.

window (windows)
n. A *window* is a sheet of glass across a hole in the wall that lets in the light.

windowsill (windowsills)
n. A *windowsill* is a shelf at the bottom of a window.

windy (windier, windiest)
adj. A *windy* place has little or no shelter from the wind.

wing (wings)

n. The *wings* of a bird or insect are the parts they use for flying.

wink (winks, winking, winked)
vb. If you *wink,* you open and close one eye very quickly.

winkle (winkles)
n. A *winkle* is a small shellfish that can be eaten.

winner (winners)
n. The *winner* of a race or a competition is the one who comes first.

a b c d e f g h i j k l m

wire (wires)

   n. Wire is a long, thin strip of metal. Wire can be used for making fences and bird cages, or it can carry an electrical current.

wise (wiser, wisest)

   adj. Someone who is *wise* knows many things.

wish (wishes, wishing, wished)

   1. *n.* A *wish* is a longing for something you have not got.
   2. *vb.* If you *wish* for something to happen, you hope it will.

witch (witches)

   n. A *witch* is a woman who uses magic. In fairy stories, *witches* fly on broomsticks and wear long pointed hats.

wobble (wobbles, wobbling, wobbled)

   vb. If you *wobble,* you shake from side to side.

woke see **wake**

wolf (wolves)

   n. A *wolf* is a wild animal that looks like a large dog.

woman (women)

   n. A *woman* is a girl who has grown up.

wombat (wombats)

   n. A *wombat* is a small furry animal that lives in Australia. *Wombats* eat plants.

won see **win**

wonder (wonders, wondering, wondered)

   vb. If you *wonder* about something, you think about it and want to know more.

wonderful

   adj. Something that is *wonderful,* fills you with a feeling of surprise and happiness.

wood

   n. Wood is the hard material from the trunks and branches of trees.

wooden

   adj. If something is *wooden,* it is made of wood.

woodland (woodlands)

   n. A *woodland* is an area of countryside covered with trees.

woodlouse (woodlice)

   n. A *woodlouse* is a small grey creature that lives in damp places.

wool

n. *Wool* is the thick, soft hair that grows on sheep. It can be spun and woven or knitted and used for making clothes.

woolly (woollier, woolliest)

   adj. Something *woolly* is made of wool.

word (words)

   n. A *word* is a sound you say, write or read, and that you understand.

wore see **wear**

work (works, working, worked)

   vb. When you *work*, you are busy doing something. Many people get paid for *working*.

worker (workers)

   n. A *worker* is someone who works.

world (worlds)

   n. The *world* is the planet we live on.

worm (worms)

   n. A *worm* is a long, thin creature that lives in the soil. *Worms* have no bones and no legs.

worn see **wear**

worry (worries, worrying, worried)

   vb. If you *worry*, you think about problems or unpleasant things that might happen.

worse see **bad**

worst see **bad**

wound (wounds, wounding, wounded)

   1. *n.* A *wound* is a cut or a hole in someone's flesh.
   2. *vb.* If you *wound* someone, you hurt them.

wrap (wraps, wrapping, wrapped)

vb. When you *wrap* something, you cover it tightly with paper or plastic.

wriggle (wriggles, wriggling, wriggled)
vb. When you *wriggle*, you twist and turn your body very quickly.

wrinkle (wrinkles)

n. A *wrinkle* is a small line in the skin.

write (writes, writing, wrote)
vb. When you *write*, you make marks or words on paper so that people can read them.

wrong

It's in your LEFT hand....

adj. If you are *wrong*, you are not right.

X-ray (X-rays)

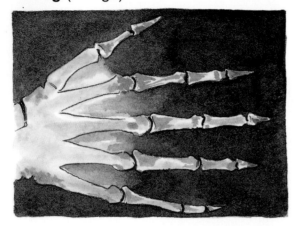

n. An *X-ray* is a special photograph that shows the inside of the body.

y

yard (yards)

n. A *yard* is a space outside a building that is usually made of concrete and has a wall around it.

yawn (yawns, yawning, yawned)

vb. When you *yawn*, you open your mouth wide and breathe in more air. You yawn because you are tired.

year (years)

n. A *year* is twelve months.

yeast (yeasts)

n. Yeast is a type of fungus that is used to make bread rise.

yell (yells, yelling, yelled)

vb. If you *yell*, you shout loudly.

yellow (yellower, yellowest)

adj. If something is *yellow*, it is the colour of daffodils and sunshine.

yesterday

n. Yesterday was the day before today.

yelp (yelps, yelping, yelped)

vb. If a dog *yelps*, it makes a short, loud cry.

yodel (yodels, yodelling. yodelled)

vb. If someone *yodels*, they make a high sound on two notes as part of a song. This type of singing comes from Switzerland.

a   b   c   d   e   f   g   h   i   j   k   l   m

yoghurt

n. Yoghurt is a creamy food made from milk. It tastes slightly sour unless it is flavoured with fruit or sugar.

young (younger, youngest)

adj. A *young* person, animal or plant has not lived very long.

your

Your things belong to you.

yourself

Yourself is you and how you are.

Z

zoo (zoos)

n. A *zoo* is a place where animals from many countries are kept so that people can watch them and study them.

zookeeper (zookeepers)

n. A *zookeeper* looks after the animals in a zoo.

Parts of Speech

The parts of speech used in this dictionary are:

n. noun   *vb.* verb   *adj.* adjective   *adv.* adverb

Noun

A *noun* names a person, a place or a thing.
Cup, mouse and *village* are all nouns.

There are usually two forms of noun. The first headword that you see tells you how to spell only one person, place or thing. This is called the *singular* form. In brackets there is the word you use when you mean more than one. This is called the *plural* form.

cup (cups)
    One *cup,* two *cups.*

mouse (mice)
    One *mouse,* two *mice.*

village (villages)
    One *village,* two *villages.*

Verb

A *verb* tells you what someone or something is doing, will do or has done. It is an action word.
Write, ride and *sneeze* are all verbs.

There are usually four forms of verbs.
sneeze (sneezes, sneezing, sneezed)

Some verbs do not follow this rule and have five forms.
write (writes, writing, written, wrote)

You use the different forms to show when something happened and who it happened to.

sneeze (sneezes, sneezing, sneezed)
I *sneeze* when I smell polish.
He *sneezes* when he has a tickle in his
    nose.
She went on *sneezing* all night.
The last time the dog *sneezed* was
    yesterday.

Adjective

An *adjective* tells you more about a noun. It is a describing word. *Happy, sad* and *beautiful* are all adjectives.

Some adjectives have three forms:
happy (happier, happiest)

With some adjectives, adding er or est does not sound right, so we use more or most in front of them:
beautiful, more beautiful, most beautiful.

He was *happy*, she was *happier* but I was *happiest*.
The painting was *beautiful*.
The tall vase was *more beautiful* than the small one.
The dawn was the *most beautiful* I had ever seen.

Adverb

An *adverb* is a word that tells you more about a verb. It tells you how someone does something.
Happily, crossly and *loudly* are all adverbs.

She sang *happily*.
The cat waved its tail *crossly*.
He shouted *loudly*.

Some adverbs tell you more about where or when something happened.
Through, then and *against* are adverbs, too.

He went *through* the hedge.
Then she sat down.
The ladder leant *against* the wall.

Days of the week

Monday   Tuesday   Wednesday   Thursday   Friday   Saturday   Sunday

Months of the year

Seasons of the year

January

February

Winter

March

Spring

April

May

June

Summer

July

August

September

Autumn

October

November

Winter

December

Numbers

1	one	**11**	eleven	**30**	thirty
2	two	**12**	twelve	**40**	forty
3	three	**13**	thirteen	**50**	fifty
4	four	**14**	fourteen	**60**	sixty
5	five	**15**	fifteen	**70**	seventy
6	six	**16**	sixteen	**80**	eighty
7	seven	**17**	seventeen	**90**	ninety
8	eight	**18**	eighteen	**100**	hundred
9	nine	**19**	nineteen	**1000**	thousand
10	ten	**20**	twenty	**1,000,000**	million

Colours

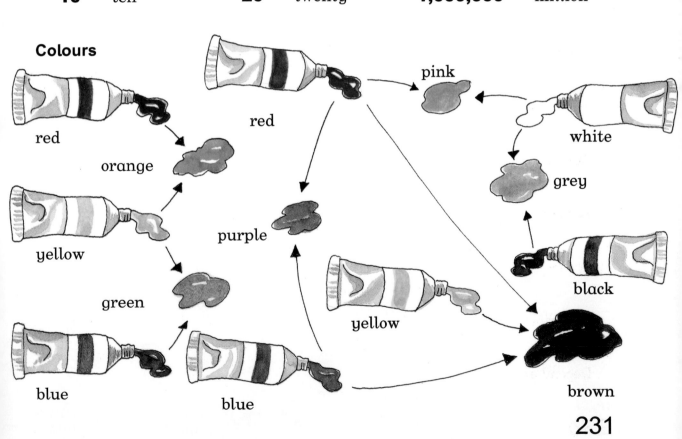

red

orange

red

pink

white

yellow

purple

grey

green

yellow

black

blue

blue

brown

Question words

how?   who?

what?   whose?

when?   which?

where?   why?

Verbs which do not follow rules

to be:

    am are is, being been, was were.

to come:

    comes, coming, came.

to go:

    goes, going, went, gone.

to do:

    does, doing, did, done.

to have:

    has, having, had.

Position words

above

on

below

up

between

behind

down

beside

over

outside

inside

in front of

against

under